PREPARED TO GIVE AN ANSWER

Developing a Biblical BIAS (Worldview)

*"But in your hearts set apart Christ as Lord. **Always be prepared to give an answer** to everyone who asks you to give the reason for the hope that you have. But do this with gentleness and respect,"*

1 Peter 3:15 NIV

Timothy V. Sanders

rora valley
PUBLISHING
www.roravalleypublishing.com

Prepared to Give an Answer by Timothy V. Sanders

©Copyright 2011, 2015 by Timothy V. Sanders and family
All Rights Reserved

Published by Rora Valley Publishing
www.roravalleypublishing.com

ISBN: 978-0-9851315-3-1

First Edition, November 2011
Second Edition (various font changes, minor content additions, revised cover),
January 2015

Cover photo: Abbi Sanders of Southern Rose Photography
Photo setting courtesy of Overall Company, Opelika, Alabama
Cover design: Elizabeth Hildreth
Editing Assistance: Lora Lynn Fanning and Noah Sanders

Dedication

To my wonderful bride Wendi and my children,
Lora Lynn, Noah, Abbi, Rebekah, Grace,
Ethan, Emanuel, Gabriel, and Nehemiah.

Thanks for your love and patience and continual encouragement.
May you continue to walk in the light of God's Truth.

Beginnings – ORIGIN   *(Where did we come from?)*
- **O**nly Two Choices
- **R**ealize the Significance
- **I**s it Faith or Science?
  - LAB - Lookable, Accessible, Breakable
- **G**uess at the Evidence
- **I**nspect the Evidence
  - Universe = "Decay"
  - Age of the Earth = "Can't Say"
  - Origin of Life by Chance = "No Way"
  - Evolution of Species and Man = "Lacks Genes and Tweens"
- **N**o Compromise
  - DON'T - <u>D</u>eath, <u>O</u>rder of Creation, <u>N</u>ames in genealogies, <u>T</u>en Commandments refer to seven-day week

Intent of Life – LIFE   *(Why are we here?)*
- **L**ove - GOD and MAN
- **I**ncrease - GROW
- **F**aithfulness - Time, Talent, Treasure
- **E**ternity – Past, Present, Future

Authority – POWER   *(Who's in charge?)*   A God Who is:
- **P**ersonal and Loving
- **O**mnipotent
- **W**ise and All-Knowing
- **E**verywhere and Eternal
- **R**ighteous and Reliable

Standards – RULES   *(What are the rules?)*   God's rules are:
- **R**evealed supernaturally, not derived by reason
- **U**niversal and apply to everyone, everywhere, all the time
- **L**oving
- **E**nforced
- **S**teadfast

CONTENTS

Preface - The Story Behind This Book 6

Introduction 9

1. Where Did We Come From? 17

2. Why Are We Here? 79

3. Who's In Charge? 133

4. What Are the Rules? 157

Conclusion 183

BIAS Review 186

Appendix A: BIAS Answers for Other Worldviews 188

Appendix B: Other Topics - Worldview Comparison Chart 190

Appendix C: Recommended Resources 192

Selected Index 194

Topic Outline 195

PREFACE - THE STORY BEHIND THIS BOOK

Is a Christian worldview reasonable, or is it illogical?

Is it possible to defend my faith against an intellectual skeptic?

When I'm told that science has disproved the Bible, what do I say?

Is biblical "faith" believing in something in spite of the evidence?

You are now holding my answers to these and related questions.

I grew up going to church, but I was an adult before I became a born-again follower of Christ. I was working at a university and was surrounded by many people more educated than me. Some of these people were skeptics who believed that biblical Christianity was not a reasonable worldview for an intelligent person. I remember the frustration I felt when I didn't have answers to objections they raised about my faith. Even professing Christian friends had rejected biblical Creation because they felt it had been disproved by science. Modern science was presented to me as proof that there was no need for a supernatural Creator, and "facts" they presented about evolution seemed to support their position. I trusted that there were answers to their objections, but I didn't know what they were. If the Bible wasn't trustworthy concerning creation, how could I trust the rest of it?

For awhile I attempted to gather my own facts so I could "win" these discussions with skeptics. That started me down the path that eventually led to this book. But after some time I realized that no matter how much I learned there would always be someone smarter than me who "knew" things I couldn't refute.

Preface - The Story Behind This Book

So my studies broadened into a study of worldviews. Did "faith" mean that I had to believe certain things in spite of overwhelming contrary evidence?

As I grew in my understanding that a biblical worldview is comprehensive, I expanded my outline from the creation/evolution topic to the other big questions about life, God, and the standards of right and wrong. I learned that the Bible provides the most logical worldview, and in this book I explain why.

A related interest of mine is the art of summarizing a large amount of important information into brief and easy-to-memorize acrostics. An acrostic organizes the first letters of the major points so that they match the letters in an existing word (such as BIAS or LIFE). When I turn ideas into acrostics they are much easier for me to recall than if they are just in some notes somewhere. The acrostics in this book allow me to carry my outline around in my head and pull out a piece as needed when I get the chance to share truths that God has showed me.

So the following is my effort to organize the basics of a biblical worldview in a way that can be memorized. This outline has helped me calmly explain to others why I have hope in Christ and why it makes sense for them to have faith in Him as well. I am no longer intimidated by "smart" people who reject God. I may not know much in comparison to all there is to know. But I also realize that someone ten times smarter than me just knows ten times almost nothing - which is still pretty close to nothing!

I originally wrote this for my family, but have been encouraged to make it available to others. I pray that it will be helpful to those who read it, and that it will encourage followers of Jesus to live their lives in light of God's truth. To be His ambassadors we need to know how to answer life's big questions according to His Word.

Preface - The Story Behind This Book

Although I intend to show why faith in God is reasonable and logical, please understand that reason alone won't convince people of the truth of God's Word. God says:

" The man without the Spirit does not accept the things that come from the Spirit of God, for they are foolishness to him, and he cannot understand them, because they are spiritually discerned." (1 Corinthians 2:14)

A man's reason cannot give him faith or an understanding of God's Word. A man must be given faith *by* God before he is able to understand the things *of* God. If this book is helpful to you, all thanks are due to God who alone can give us true wisdom.

To God be the glory,

Timothy V. Sanders

INTRODUCTION

WHO, ME? BIASED?

*"**Bias**: a mental leaning or inclination; partiality; prejudice; bent"* (Webster's)

If you think being biased is a bad thing, take a deep breath and hold it before you read the next sentence.......

You are biased. So am I. So is everyone in the world.

(You can breathe now - the hard part is over.)

In the movie "The Pistol," Pete Maravich's father holds up a basketball and a pen to illustrate to his team why they need to listen to him. "This ball represents everything there is to know about the great game of basketball." He draws a small circle on the ball. "That's everything I know about basketball". He then makes a dot. "That's everything you know about basketball."

Great illustration.

It's also a great illustration about life and the worldview each of us has. Imagine a ball that represents everything there is to know about everything in life for all of the past, present, and future. How big a circle on the ball would represent your knowledge? How big a circle would represent the smartest person you know?

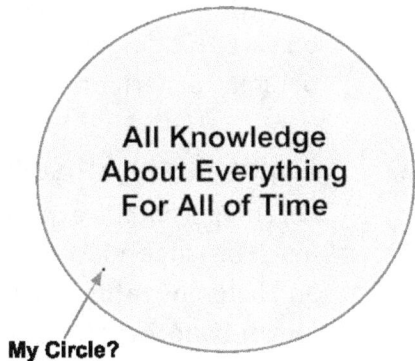

All Knowledge About Everything For All of Time

My Circle?

Introduction

None of us knows everything. Most of us are honest enough to admit that relative to "all knowledge from all time" our little dot couldn't even be seen on the ball. Yet that doesn't keep us from having opinions about the whole ball. As humans there are certain questions we can't help but ask about our lives. Here are four "whole ball" questions for which we each have an opinion:

1. **Where did we come from?**
2. **Why are we here?**
3. **Who's in charge?**
4. **What are the rules?**

Sources of Our Opinions

So how do we each come up with our answers? There's really only three sources for any opinions and answers we have:

1. ### Personal experience and observations

   If we have personal experience with an area of knowledge then we have a first-hand basis for our opinion. We all know about gravity because we experience it daily (especially as we get older). But in the few years we have on earth we don't have enough time to **know** much by personal experience.

2. ### Experiences/observations of other people

   Learning from the experiences of others lets us draw from a much broader pool of knowledge. Our education, reading, and listening brings us much second-hand (or third-hand, fourth-hand, etc.) knowledge that is filtered from the first-hand experiences of others. When someone we like or respect tells us their opinion based on their experience with a subject, we often adopt their opinion as our own. This is easier than having no opinion on subjects for which we have no first-hand knowledge. This is a very useful source but still leaves us with a very small dot on the ball.

3. ## Our Personal Bias about the rest of the ball

Our bias (you can substitute the word "worldview" if it sounds better) is how we arrive at opinions about the rest of the ball of knowledge that we can't cover with first-hand or second-hand knowledge. And, for even the most educated and intelligent of us, our bias is the basis for our opinions on 99.99+ percent of the ball. Don't believe it? Look at the four questions above and think about who has first-hand knowledge to answer any of them.

That's why it is <u>necessary</u> for each of us to be biased. If I don't have a bias I have no way to form opinions about most of life and the world around me. My "mental leaning or inclination" (as Webster puts it) gives me a basis for having opinions about things I can't personally verify by experience. If we were earthworms we might not need a bias since we might not have any opinions about anything - we care only about the dirt we live in and experience. But we are human beings with minds that seek answers to things above and beyond our "dirt."

THE "BEST" BIAS

Since your bias (worldview) is so important, how do you know if you have the best one or the "right" one? How do you even know if there is a right one?

This seems like a hard question to answer, but our choices are pretty limited (as in two). Either my answers to life's big questions are based on my Reasoning ("truth" as determined by my intellect), or they are based on Revelation (truth as revealed to me by One who knows the truth) :

1. ## Based on Reasoning

   If the only source of answers is my evaluation of input from my experiences and from other biased people, all biases are equally valid and none is better or more right than any other. If you choose to believe this answer then it doesn't really matter which bias you choose. It would also be wrong of you to ever tell anyone else that his/her worldview was "wrong." Some opinions may be more educated and well-reasoned than others, but they are all based on imperfect knowledge. In this choice you are saying that your Reason and Intellect are your highest authority, and you use them to judge all ideas and to determine "Truth" (even though you know almost nothing of the ball).

2. ## Based on Revelation

   If there is One who does know everything (the whole ball), basing my bias on His knowledge would be the best and only rational choice. This option is easier to accept once you admit that you personally don't have all the knowledge needed to be sure of most things. In this choice I'm saying that the only things I know for sure are those things that are Revealed to me. But if there is no one who knows the whole ball I'm stuck with option one.

I believe there is One who knows everything about everything past, present, and future. He claims to have provided us with some of His first-hand knowledge in the Bible. If you and I accept His testimony then we should base our worldview bias on what He says. If we don't accept His testimony then we're stuck with our own imperfect guesses.

Introduction

Therefore this book uses a "presuppositional" approach to answering life's big questions. I "presuppose" that the best source of truthful answers is the One who knows all answers and has given us some of that knowledge in the Bible. I still use the reasoning ability He has given me, but if my reason doesn't understand something He says, I'm going to assume He's right. He's the one that knows the whole ball – my "reasoning" tells me that it's illogical to make MY knowledge be the final judge of truth.

JESUS AND THE BIBLE

A Christian worldview is built on the cornerstone of Jesus Christ with His Word, the Bible, as the foundation. *If you want to know how a Christian worldview is different from all others in the world, the simplest answer is: Jesus.* The Bible teaches that Jesus is both the eternal Son of God (100% God) and the only perfect man (100% man) who willingly died for the sins and lives of His People. All other worldviews reject Jesus as being God and/or reject faith in Him as being the only way to be reconciled to God. Colossians 1:16 says that "all things were created by him and for him", so everything in this book is ultimately about Jesus.

Jesus is also God's Word (John 1:1, Hebrews 1:1-2). We know who Jesus is and what He has done only because of God's Word to us, the Bible. Without the Bible we would not know much of anything (just our little dot on the whole ball). So the foundation of our Christian worldview is the Bible. *The Bible is God's written communication to us that answers the whole-ball questions we could not answer ourselves.*

NOTE:

> In the "Revealed" section in the RULES chapter we examine why we have confidence that the Bible is God's Word. You might want to read that section first if you have questions about the Bible's trustworthiness.

DO NOT ANSWER A FOOL.....

In Proverbs 26:4-5 there is a puzzling statement: *"Do not answer a fool according to his folly, or you will be like him yourself. Answer a fool according to his folly, or he will be wise in his own eyes."* One possible application of this passage is that it outlines the ground rules for discussions of worldview topics. The first verse of the passage can remind us **"don't concede/agree that we are capable of determining ultimate truth via human reasoning."** We should establish at the beginning of any conversation that the only reliable source of truth is the One who knows everything (and that's not either of us).

The second verse could be paraphrased **"if a person rejects God's truth, show him the logical implications of his position."** If God does not exist, then our logic is the random result of synapses firing in a brain that evolved through a series of accidents without any intelligent design. This would make our logic totally unreliable. Our ability to even ponder the question of God is totally dependent on a brain that has been designed. In a "matter-is-all-there-is" worldview there is no logic in depending on logic. You may protest that your brain works perfectly well, but where did you get your standard? Unless there is an ultimate <u>source</u> of logic we have no grounds for saying we are "rational" while another man is insane.

But in all our conversations with others we need to obey God's command to give our reasons with "gentleness and respect". Any knowledge we have was given us by God, so our conversations should convey humility and thankfulness rather than arrogance or self-righteousness.

For who makes you different from anyone else? What do you have that you did not receive? And if you did receive it, why do you boast as though you did not? (1 Corinthians 4:7)

WHAT THIS BOOK COVERS

The following chapters provide an outline for building a Biblical BIAS based on the Word of God who claims to know everything. The outline is arranged as an acrostic using the word **BIAS** to present answers to the four "whole ball" questions about life presented above.

B   <u>B</u>eginnings (ORIGIN acrostic) - *Where did we come from?*

I   <u>I</u>ntent (LIFE acrostic) - *Why are we here?*

A   <u>A</u>uthority (POWER acrostic) - *Who's in charge?*

S   <u>S</u>tandards (RULES acrostic) - *What are the rules?*

This book is written to accomplish three objectives:

1. *A Sufficient Worldview Overview…*

To provide a sufficient (not exhaustive) presentation of a biblical worldview that can help a Christian easily compare/contrast this view with other worldviews. This is intended to be an easily-read overview rather than a detailed reference book.

2. *…That Upholds Faith as Reasonable…*

To give reasons why a Biblical worldview faith is at least as intellectually sound as the faith of the most educated follower of any other worldview.

3. *…And Can Be Memorized via Acrostics.*

To organize the outline systematically so that it can be memorized using acrostics. If you don't carry a clear worldview in your head and heart you won't be ready to "give a reason for the hope that is within you" when God gives you the opportunity.

The result of having a systematic, memorized outline for our biblical worldview is that we are prepared:

*"But in your hearts set apart Christ as Lord. **Always be prepared to give an answer** to everyone who asks you to give the reason for the hope that you have. But do this with gentleness and respect,"*

1 Peter 3:15 NIV

HOW THIS BOOK IS ORGANIZED

The chapters in this book follow the BIAS outline and the supporting acrostics that are listed in the front of this book. Each chapter addresses one of the four worldview questions. The page headings identify which of the four questions is being answered and which point is being discussed within each acrostic. The Topic Outline at the end of the book also provides a roadmap for the material covered.

I believe my outline is consistent with God's teaching, but encourage you to be like the Bereans in Paul's time and "examine the Scriptures to see if what is said is true." (adapted from Acts 17:11) Let's begin......

"The fear of the Lord is the beginning of knowledge......" *Proverbs 1:7a*

1. WHERE DID WE COME FROM?

<u>B</u>eginnings - A Question of O.R.I.G.I.N.

Our first big question is "where did we come from and how did we get here?" Are we here for any reason? Are we an insignificant blob of matter that is the result of millions of accidents over billions of years? Do we have a Creator? Is there really a Force that will be with us in our battle against the Death Star and the evil Galactic Empire (for those of you who saw the Star Wars movies)?

To guide us through our discussion of this question we'll use the acrostic "O.R.I.G.I.N." so we can organize and remember the major points. We'll have other acrostics to outline supporting points. The major points in this discussion are:

- **<u>O</u>**nly Two Choices
- **<u>R</u>**ealize the Significance
- **<u>I</u>**s it Faith or Science?
- **<u>G</u>**uess at the Evidence
- **<u>I</u>**nspect the Evidence
- **<u>N</u>**o Compromise

O - Only Two Choices

How many possible answers are there to the question of our origin? It may seem that there are a lot of different answers floating around in the world. But from a broad perspective there are actually only two:

1.   *Either God created all of space, time, the universe, us, and everything else just as He said in the Bible, or...*

2.   *We don't know for sure!* (It could have been evolution, natural processes, aliens, cosmic forces, etc.)

If you think I've oversimplified the options, remember the basketball illustration from the introduction. What knowledge would be required to answer the question of where we come from? I'm not talking about a guess, I'm talking about <u>knowing</u> the answer to the question. We can only know for sure where we came from if there was a reliable witness who recorded what happened. If you don't think there were any witnesses then you'll have to be content with your guesses or someone else's guesses. If you think God is a reliable witness to what He did then it would be foolish to believe any other explanation.

Other non-biblical religions have stories about origins or creation, and some of them have similarities to the biblical account. But the Bible is the book whose writings claim to have been directed and inspired directly by God, the Creator. This means that it claims to be an eyewitness account rather than a "story" or legend (see the "Revealed" discussion in the RULES chapter).

Right now you might be thinking that the question of origins falls into the realm of science and that I'm ignoring proven scientific facts. Be patient. We'll talk about science after our next point.

R - REALIZE THE SIGNIFICANCE

OK. Let's say you concede that there are only two real answers to the question of origin. Is it really that important what you believe about where we came from?

YES, IT IS IMPORTANT!! Your answer to this question is vital to everything you believe and do and hope. Why? Because:

If God created as He said He did, He owns us and He has the right to say what's right and wrong

If God did not create us, no one owns us and no one has the right to say what's right and wrong

If God owns us He can tell us what is RIGHT and what is WRONG whether we like it or not. We can choose to do things that He says are wrong, but we can't change the fact that they _are_ wrong. We can choose to do something He says is right and it will be right even if everyone else thinks it is wrong.

On the other hand, if God did not create us as He said then there are no fixed standards for right and wrong. Certainly there are laws and customs that we decide and enforce, but they are always subject to being changed by the next generation of people in power. The rules can continually change because no one has the power to make them ultimate and final. In this scenario all standards of right and wrong are simply opinions.

Do you see why this is such a vital question? Our daily decisions about what we do and don't do revolve around our sense of right and wrong. If someone offends you is it okay for you to pull out a gun and shoot him/her? Why or why not? Where did you get that idea? If you thought you wouldn't get caught and decided to shoot would that make it OK if you got away with it? Would it be OK in a different time period or in a different country?

Let's look at a few questions to demonstrate the significance of whether God or man establishes the standard for right and wrong:

If Person A's life is inconveniencing me, is it okay for me to end Person A's life if I have the opportunity?
This is the question we face today on issues such as abortion, euthanasia (a sanitized word meaning "good death", presumably from the perspective of someone still living), starvation of handicapped infants, medical decisions to refuse care to the elderly, and others.

- **If God owns us,** He says that He is the author of life and except for capital punishment, self-defense, or war He does not condone the killing of people (who are made in His image). One of the earliest sins recorded in Genesis is the sin of murder where Cain killed Abel.
- **If God doesn't own us** then we have no standard of right and wrong, just opinions that we think best serve our interests. Presumably the stronger (politically, militarily, financially) will enforce their opinions on the weaker. The younger stronger generation may decide to do away with the elderly because they cost too much to keep. But that cost doesn't seem too high when they themselves grow older and find that they now are no longer the "strong." If Reason is your source of authority *your opinion of whether it is right to kill the less useful people will depend on whether you are one of them.* But it will still be only an opinion and you have no reasonable basis for saying anything is "wrong." All you can say is whether you like it.

Why do people get married?

Is marriage just tradition? Why is marriage necessary when you can just live with someone?

- **If God owns us**, God says in Genesis that He instituted marriage so that man would not be alone and so that husband and wife can become one. Later He tells us that marriage is also to produce godly offspring and to model the relationship between Christ and His Bride, the Church. Marriage between one man and one woman for life is the only sanctioned union.

- **If God doesn't own us**, we can make up our own rules about marriage. Many people today (including many in our government) are rejecting the idea that marriage is the only right way for a man and woman to join lives. If no one owns us and has the right to establish right and wrong then this is a logical conclusion. Why don't we change the definition of marriage to include any type of live-in arrangement? Why does it have to involve a man and a woman? If you can get enough people to agree with you to make it legal then you can enforce your opinions on everyone. You can even force employers to pay for medical benefits for any type of "marriage" partner. The thing you can't really do is say that it's "right" since that would imply an absolute standard which you say doesn't exist.

Why do we have to wear clothes?

Many people probably haven't thought much about this question. The concept of modesty is falling out of favor. In the U.S. we hear of legal attacks to protect "free speech" if an organization tries to establish any dress code related to modesty.

- **If God owns us**, we need to wear clothes that cover the private parts of our bodies. God gave clothing to Adam and Eve as a covering for sin in Genesis. Because of our sin nature, nakedness produces lustful thoughts and destroys modesty and purity.

- **If God doesn't own us**, there is no absolute standard from God and we're just left with opinions about clothes. If you say "so what?" then think how you would react when your co-workers, neighbors, children's teachers, plumber, etc., stop wearing clothes. With at least some of them you would probably want to say "that's not ri....." but you would have to bite your tongue on that last word since you don't own them and can't tell them what's "right".

These and many other examples illustrate why the question of where we came from is so foundational to how we think. If we reject the notion of a Creator Who owns us, we are also rejecting the notion of any absolute rights or wrongs in the world because there is no one to set the standards. No absolutes may sound good if I think it gives me freedom, but no limits on what <u>others</u> can do is not a comforting thought! *Without a Creator we can argue about preferences but we can't insist on justice.*

Genesis and Christian Ethics

Another reason the question of origins is so important is that Genesis is a cornerstone of the Bible and Christian morality. If Genesis is not reliable, major doctrines of our faith have no foundation. Here is a list I compiled from Ken Ham's <u>The Genesis Record</u> of some biblical doctrines that rely on the assumption that the book of Genesis is a reliable account:

BIBLICAL DOCTRINES BASED ON GENESIS

1. God was "in the beginning" and is eternal (Gen 1:1, 21:33)
2. God is the Creator of the universe and everything (Gen 1)
3. Creation is not ongoing; God completed it (Gen 2:1-2)
4. God created both male and female (Gen 1:27; 5:2)
5. All human beings are descendants of Adam and Eve (Gen 1:28a, 3:20)
6. Man is not an animal; he was set above the animals (Gen 1:26-28, 2:19)
7. We are made in the "image of God" (Gen 1:27, 5:1) and we have a soul (Gen 2:7)
8. There is good, and there is evil (Gen 2:16-17, 3:5, 22)
9. God is holy and righteous
10. The original world was a paradise; "very good" (Gen 1:31)
11. Humans were originally sinless
12. Humans originally walked with God (Gen 3:8) and had a much closer and more direct relationship with the Creator.
13. God works in human affairs and has from the beginning.
14. God sets laws that we are to obey (e.g. Gen 26:5)
15. God sees all of our sins and has done so from the beginning (Gen 3:11, 4:10, 6:5, etc.)
16. The circumstances of the first sinful act of man (the test and temptation of "the tree of the knowledge of good and evil") are explained in Genesis
17. The sin of our original parents, Adam and Eve, is the reason why all humans are born sinful; the sin nature is passed from generation to generation
18. **Sin separated man from God** (Gen 3:24)
19. God punishes sin (Gen 3:14-19, 4:11-12, 6:5-7, etc.)
20. Man's sin and God's curse began the corruption and decay of paradise (Gen 3:17, 22-23). The Fall and God's curse are ultimate reasons why our world today is imperfect - filled with problems, suffering, and evils, both physical and moral.
21. **Death came through sin** (Gen 3:19 - see also Rom 5:12)
22. The origin of God's plan to save man
23. Woman is of the man (Gen 2:22-23)
24. Woman is for the man (Gen 2:18)
25. "Leave father and mother..." (Gen 2:24)
26. United husband and wife "become one flesh" (Gen 2:24)
27. Male headship in the normal marriage relationship (Gen 3:16)
28. Sinfulness of homosexuality and other sexual perversions (e.g. Gen 18:20, 19:4-6, 13)
29. Origin of the "chosen people" - Abraham and his descendants (Gen 12:1, etc.)

SOME OTHER IMPLICATIONS OF EVOLUTIONARY THOUGHT
The fruit of evolutionary thought has had far-reaching implications.
Here are a few:

Racism

Men have used evolution as an excuse for racism by claiming that
people who are different from them are less evolved and therefore
inferior. Whether it's white versus black, Aryan versus Jew, or
European versus pygmy, evolution gives justification to those who
want to consider themselves superior beings. ***God says*** *that we are
all one race, all descended from Adam and from Noah.*

Education Methods

In the late 19th century G. Stanley Hall developed the idea of age-
segregated education based on Darwinism and Ernst Haeckel's
now-disproved theory of recapitulation. John Dewey built on this
to create our modern education model that produces people who
think they are (and often act like) animals. Dewey was an atheist
who wanted to destroy the influence of Christian homes. ***God
teaches*** *that education is to be parent-directed, age-integrated, and
focused on developing people who honor the fact that they are
specially made in God's image.*

Social Darwinism

In the late 19th century people began to apply the "survival of the
fittest" concept to business, nations, sports and other areas of life.
This became a convenient excuse for imposing your interests
mercilessly on someone else – "it's just natural that the strong
survive and the weak die." This concept is so prevalent today that
we often don't even recognize how unbiblical our "competitive"
natures can be. ***God says*** *that we are to treat others as we want to
be treated, protect the weak, help those in need, and consider the
interests of others ahead of our own.*

Evolutionary Law

For much of past history most judicial systems practiced under a system of justice based on common law and the original intent of a law. Judges and courts generally administered justice based on a "higher law", an accepted standard of right and wrong. The Bible and biblical morality were often quoted and used in trials and decisions. ***God says*** *that we are to judge fairly (by His standards), to protect the innocent, and to defend the rights of the poor and needy.*

Beginning in the late 19th century law schools started to teach a form of law based on evolutionary principles. This became known as "case law" and was based on the concept that law needs to "evolve" in order to reflect our evolving state of higher intelligence. This radically changed the practice of law and turned it into a competition "where the smartest/strongest wins" instead of the pursuit of true justice.

- Rather than referring to some fixed, absolute, biblical, and moral standard we now use decisions from previous cases (precedents) as the basis for our decisions in order to achieve an "ever-evolving" standard of justice.

- Rather than worrying about what was originally intended when interpreting a contractual agreement such as the Constitution, we reinterpret it to mean whatever we think it should mean so that it "evolves" with changes in current thinking.

    - Suppose I had a signed agreement with you. Then later I told you that the contract now means whatever I say it says. You would say that's wrong. Yet that's exactly what the federal government has done with the limits placed on it by the Constitution.

Be Watchful......

Evolution-based concepts have infiltrated many areas of our lives since their promotion by Charles Darwin. As Christians we need to:

- Recognize that these concepts are anti-biblical
- Recognize that evolution is a belief system that is supported not by science but by a preference for self-rule over God rule
- Be prepared to explain why these concepts are not supported by reason so that others can gain confidence in rejecting these ideas as dangerous and foolish.

Trustworthiness of Scripture

The most significant question about origins is this: are we going to believe what God said or are we going to imitate Satan and say "did God really say?" If we don't trust the Bible in the first chapter, why should we trust the rest of it? It seems to me that we have to trust Gods "revelation" about origins or we're choosing to elevate our "reason" as a judge over God's Word. As we showed in the introduction, our little dot of knowledge is a pitiful resource to use to judge the Author and Ruler of the Universe.

"OK, so I see the significance of this issue, but....."

Can a rational person really believe in creation today?
> YES! In the next few points we'll apply rational thought to the question of our origins.

Hasn't science proven that we are a product of evolution?
> NO! In the next point we'll discover why neither creation nor evolution is capable of being "proven by science" as the source of our existence.

I - IS IT FAITH OR SCIENCE?

Most of us raised in Western civilization have been instilled with a profound respect for science. We've seen amazing results and advances from modern science that make our lives easier, healthier, and less boring. Scientists have provided us with insight into many complex issues that were not even dreamed of in previous generations (at least as far as we know). In many ways science and technology can be viewed as the king and queen of modern civilization because they rule much of our lives.

When it comes to answering the question of our origins it is logical for us to turn to science for answers. ***However, in this case of explaining singular events in the past, science doesn't know any more than the rest of us.***

In the dictionary we get the following definition of science:

"Science - Systematized knowledge derived from observation, study, and experimentation carried on in order to determine the nature or principles of what is being studied" (Webster's)

The scientific method has to do with observing, studying, and experimenting in order to derive or prove a principle about the object of the study. The primary founders of this approach were actually Bible-believing men and women who saw themselves as pursuing insights into the marvelous order of the created universe. Science would be impossible unless there is order and a pattern to the universe. Here are just a few of the early scientists who developed the theory of science because they believed God had created order in the universe:

- Francis Bacon (1561–1626) Scientific method.
- Galileo Galilei (1564–1642) Physics, Astronomy
- Johann Kepler (1571–1630) Scientific astronomy
- Blaise Pascal (1623–1662) Hydrostatics; Barometer
- Robert Boyle (1627–1691) Chemistry; Gas dynamics
- Isaac Newton (1642–1727) Dynamics; Calculus; Gravitation law; Reflecting telescope; Spectrum of light

To be scientific, a theory or concept must have characteristics that can be remembered using the acrostic L.A.B.:

Lookable - the object of the theory or concept must be observable, something you can see (I know "lookable" is an odd word, but it helps you remember)

Available - the object of the theory or concept must be available today for study

Breakable - it must be possible to devise tests that would disprove the theory or concept

1. Where Did We Come From?   ORIGIN – Is it Faith or Science?

Using this acrostic let's examine the "Scientific" nature of Creation and Evolution:

	Theory of Special Creation	Theory of Evolution
Is it **L**ookable (can we observe it happening?)	**NO** Creation was a one-time event	**NO** The origin of the universe, of life, and of everything is an event of the past
Is it **A**vailable (can we bring it in for study today?)	**NO** Creation was a one-time event	**NO** The origin of the universe, of life, and of everything is an event of the past
Is it **B**reakable (can we disprove that it did happen?)	**NO** Creation was a one-time event	**NO** The origin of the universe, of life, and of everything is an event of the past

Neither Creation nor Evolution is a scientific theory, so they must be evaluated as belief systems.
Those who believe in either system do so by <u>faith</u>, not by science.

Two Categories of Science

We need to distinguish between two general categories of what is called "science":

- Operational Science – This is the study of how things operate and function and the development of new technologies and ideas based on what we observe. This meets the definition of true science, and nearly everyone can agree on the value of operational science research and development.

- Origins "Science" – This is the study of how the world originated and got to be in its present state. This falls outside the realm of science since theories about what happened in the past are not observable, available, or disprovable.

	Operational Science	**Origins "Science"**
Based on:	The senses (we assume they are reliable)	Assumptions about the past
Research method:	Experiments	Extrapolation - assuming the past was like the present
Deals with:	The present	The past
Results in:	Repeatable conclusions, technology	Non-repeatable stories about the past

Just like the adults in the children's story <u>The Emperor's New Clothes</u>, we're afraid to say "the emperor has no clothes" or "science can't prove anything about the past" for fear of ridicule. But the fact is that unobserved events in the past are no more a suitable topic for scientists than an explanation of DNA structure is a suitable topic for historians. Perhaps you think that I'm ignoring the many elegant theories put forth by scientists to explain how events happened in the past. We'll get to those theories, but the point I'm making here is that ***these theories fall outside of the realm of science***. Since we can't look at, study, or experiment on those origin events they are not scientifically provable or disprovable.

Origins happened in the past, and the past is not observable today.

Here's an illustration. Let's say you found what looked like a hubcap in the ditch beside a road. If you asked the question "how did the hubcap get here," how could we use science to get the answer? We would probably assume that it fell off of a car. We could call in experts who could try to compute the speed, age, model, and direction of the car that lost the hubcap. They could give us general averages and tendencies for this type of hubcap and research how many similar hubcaps have ever been found in ditches like this one. But what do we really KNOW about how that particular hubcap got there? The hubcap could have been tossed out of the back of a pickup, dropped from an airplane, spontaneously generated from chemicals in the ditch, carried there by a giant packrat, planted there by aliens, or be the fossil remains of a primitive auto plant. We can make an educated guess, but unless a reliable witness steps forth and explains what he observed we can't KNOW how it got there.

So, is this a cop-out? Is this an attempt to avoid the scientific evidence and say that everyone can believe what they want and we're all okay?

No. We have minds and we need to use them. There is evidence in the world today that we can examine to see if it is consistent with our belief. The point we're making here is that none of us can say we've "proved" creation or evolution via science. Once we've established that fact, we can approach the evidence we see in the world as "seekers" and see how well the evidence matches up with our beliefs.

The man who believes in the Creator can take heart from the first chapter of the book of Romans:

For since the creation of the world God's invisible qualities--his eternal power and divine nature--have been clearly seen, being understood from what has been made, so that men are without excuse.
Romans 1:20

This tells us that there is enough evidence of the Creator in the creation so that no one can miss it. The man who denies the Creator has to deny this evidence and look for other answers.

THE BIAS OF NATURALISM AND MATERIALISM

One major assertion of those who oppose the concept of creation is that true science is limited to naturalistic and materialistic explanations. They point out that any supernatural explanations such as God are not scientific. To some extent that is true - God can't be tested according to scientific principles.

But the fallacy in this assertion is the ridiculous notion that the limit of science is also the limit of truth.

The statement "God is not scientifically verifiable" is a very different proposition than the statement "only scientifically verifiable explanations can be true." At that point science becomes religious. A man may choose to say that he wants to consider only ideas that he can examine scientifically, but that has nothing to do with truth. It is important for Christians to realize that truth and science are not equivalent terms (real science may reveal truth, but there is truth that can't be revealed by science).

We can sum up this faulty naturalistic/materialistic line of thinking as follows:

- Everything that exists is natural and material
- We exist, so we must have come from a natural/material source
- Special creation is not natural/material so it must be false even if there is evidence to support this theory
- Evolution (molecules to man) is natural/material so it is preferable to creation even if the evidence doesn't support it

G - GUESS AT THE EVIDENCE

Before we start looking at scientific evidence for our origins let's answer the question "what would we expect to see?". This helps focus our attention on the important points. We can't inspect the past but we can look at evidence today to see whether it supports what we think happened in the past. We will:
1. Guess what evidence we should see if a theory is true
2. Examine the available evidence
3. Conclude whether the evidence supports the theory

Remember that we can't prove or disprove either theory, but we can test our personal belief system against the available evidence.

If the biblical account of Creation is true then the available evidence should fit the theory of Creation. If Evolution is true then the available evidence should fit the theory of Evolution.

EXPECTATIONAL VERSUS EVIDENTIAL

I'm going to label this concept of inspecting the evidence based on predetermined guesses as an ***"expectational"*** approach. That means we establish expectations for what evidence we should find for a particular model or theory (based on its acknowledged "bias") and then evaluate the evidence to see how well it fits. In scientific terminology our "expectational" approach is similar to proposing a theory or hypothesis and then conducting experiments to see if they support our theory.

A less effective approach (and particularly inappropriate for a study of the past) is the "evidential" approach where we try to show how we can derive the correct model solely from our intellectual review of the evidence existing today. In other words, the evidential approach says that an objective look at the "facts" will lead us to truth.

The evidential approach usually just leads to argument since our inevitable presuppositions (bias) affect even how we interpret the evidence. For example, when examining common characteristics of two creatures, a creationist sees a "common Designer" while an evolutionist sees a "common ancestor". They see the same "facts," but because of their bias they will arrive at different interpretations and different conclusions.

Although many well-intentioned people try to use the evidential approach to convince evolutionists of the truth of creation, this concept has two major flaws:

1. The evidential approach incorrectly elevates "reason" as the highest authority since we're saying that our reason will lead us to truth. As we discussed in the introduction, our reason is hopelessly inadequate because it is finite AND because the whole ball of knowledge is so vast.
2. All "facts" are interpreted by our bias, so there is no such thing as a truly "objective" look at the evidence.

WHAT WE EXPECT TO FIND

The table below summarizes what each belief system would generally "expect" we'd find in the evidence:

If Biblical Creation is true ...	If Evolution is true ...
If we believe God created the world as described in the Bible we would expect to find evidence of: <ul><li>A sudden complete creation of the universe, the world, and all living things</li><li>A time of creation within the last 6,000 to 10,000 years (based on Bible genealogy)</li><li>A worldwide flood that wiped out most life on land</li><li>No fossils indicating that one species of life evolved into another – God made each creature and "kind" fully formed</li></ul>	If we believe that the world and all creatures were created by evolution we would expect to find evidence of: <ul><li>A very slow formation of the universe and the world</li><li>A very slow development of life on earth spanning billions of years</li><li>Progressive complexity of fossilized creatures – the oldest fossils would be very simple life forms and complex life forms would not have appeared until millions of years later</li><li>Transitional fossils that show one species of life evolving into another species</li></ul>

Now that we know what we're looking for, let's look at the evidence. Again, we're not trying to prove or disprove either theory. We're simply seeing which theory about the past is most consistent with the evidence we can observe today.

I - INSPECT THE EVIDENCE

To approach this systematically we'll look individually at five major areas of evidence about our origins.

1.   Origin and Age of the Universe
2.   Age of the Earth
3.   Life from non-living matter
4.   Complex animals from simple life
5.   Man from animals

NATURE OF THE UNIVERSE

Before we get into the evidence found on earth we'll first examine the evidence found outside of the earth. Since the earth is part of the universe, the origin of the universe should help us understand the origin of the earth. Here are the expectations:

Creationist Expectation	Evolutionist Expectation
1. **The universe had a beginning.** Time, space, and matter were spoken into being at the same instant. 2. **The creation process is finished.** Creation consisted of processes that are no longer in effect.	1. **The universe has always been in existence** or had a natural origin. 2. **The processes that we currently observe should explain the origin of the universe.**

The Evidence

Probably the two most accepted "laws" of how the universe works are the 1st and 2nd Laws of Thermodynamics. These are really just generalizations that agree with all scientific data and observation we currently have, and they haven't been "proven" in a strict sense.

However, the tremendous amount of supporting evidence makes these two of the primary examples of scientific laws.

a.   The first law states that energy can be transferred to another place or transformed to another form, ***but energy can be neither created nor destroyed.*** The law does not state **why** this is so or **how** the original energy was created, but the law itself is always observed.

b.   The second law states that ***the universe is constantly getting more disorderly***. Everything is deteriorating, and useful energy is being turned into non-useful energy. Again, there is no scientific explanation of why.

What Does the Evidence Indicate?

We can sum up this evidence with the word **"DECAY"**. The universe is in a state of decay.

Creationist Interpretation

The first law of thermodynamics seems to fit the Creation model very well. On the sixth day God finished Creation. He had set the laws of the cosmos in motion. God created the initial energy, and when He finished Creation no more energy was created and none was destroyed.

The second law also fits with Creation. Because in "nature" things go from orderly to disorderly there must initially have been an "Orderliness" as a starting point. Complex systems could only be created by systems with a higher complexity. Complex man could only have been created by a more complex God.

The second law also implies that the universe is disintegrating or dying. Unless there was a Creation at a point in time the universe should already be dead (it would not cease to exist, but all the useful energy would be depleted). If it were infinitely old it would already be dead. And the decay is consistent with the Bible's teaching that all of creation was affected by sin and won't be "liberated from its bondage of decay" (Romans 8:21) until God restores it in the future.

Evolutionist Interpretation

It appears that evolutionists ignore the implications of the first law. According to their presupposition the universe has always existed (saying there was a "big bang" simply skirts the issue of the ultimate beginning), and the first law indicates that the universe has always had the same amount of energy. Evolution ignores the question of where this energy came from.

The second law is directly opposed to evolution. Evolution says that systems build themselves up into more complex and orderly forms; this is the direct opposite of what the law states.

The eternal existence of the universe is also denied by this law:

- The first law says that the universe is a "closed" system which cannot rejuvenate itself
- Evolution denies the existence of a Rejuvenator who could change the universe
- The second law states that an eternally old universe would have already disintegrated

Evolutionists try to deal with these problems by coming up with theories on how the "laws" do not apply all the time:

- The Steady State theory proposed that somewhere in unobservable space there is matter and energy being created out of nothing to balance out the observable decay of the universe. Since unobservable space has nothing to do with science, this theory has been abandoned.

- The currently popular Big Bang theory proposes that at an unobservable point in time all matter and energy were exploded into existence and into complex organization. *Then* the laws of thermodynamics took effect. There are several problems with this theory, but the most obvious is the second law - explosions produce disorder, not order.

Ingenious evolutionists have tried to address this problem by proposing that the "cosmic egg" of the Big Bang was highly complex, complex enough to create an orderly universe even after the explosion. Again, there is no plausible explanation of how this egg came into being.

Some have proposed that the universe is in a continual cycle of "banging", contracting into a universe egg, and exploding again. Even if one can somehow picture how the collapse of the universe can produce order, there is not enough mass in the universe for gravity to pull it together.

In spite of these problems leading "scientists" still stand by the Big Bang theory. Isaac Asimov acknowledged that the facts are against the theory, but stated that he had a "hunch" that we'll find new evidence to support it (Morris, Biblical Basis of Modern Science pg. 152*). It's hard not to get the impression that some men will accept any idea as long as it is an alternative to believing in God.*

Related Topics

"If Creation took place only a few thousand years ago as taught in the Bible, how has light from stars millions of light years away reached us?"

Remember that light years are a measure of *distance*, not of time. The simplest explanation is that God made the stars "full grown" with their light paths immediately (supernaturally) established. The Bible says that the lights were made to serve as signs, and it only makes sense that they would have been visible to Adam and Eve on their first night in the garden.

Some creation scientists object to the simple answer because it means that the events we witness from (supposedly) millions of light years away (exploding stars, formation of stars, etc.) didn't really happen. I don't have as much problem with that because it seems to me that all things God originally made would have "appeared" older than they were. But here are a couple other plausible scientific explanations that have also been proposed:

- The speed of light may have decreased, and light initially had an exceedingly high velocity.
- Another theory uses a type of geometry that suggests light travels in a curved space called Riemannian space, and light in such a space could be seen from anywhere in the universe in less than sixteen years.

"Aren't our sun and solar system and planet fairly ordinary in the universe?"

NOT AT ALL. There is such fine tuning for Earth's situation that even atheists acknowledge that the odds of our conditions occurring by chance are astronomical (pun intended ☺).

Here are some examples[1]:

- Our sun is the right color. If it was redder or bluer, photosynthesis would be less efficient.
- Our sun is the right mass. If it was larger there would be too much radiation and if it was smaller the earth would have to be closer to it (and more affected by its gravity).
- The earth's distance from the sun is crucial for:
  - A stable water cycle. Too far away, and most water would freeze; too close and most water would boil.
  - Temperatures that support life.
- Gravity, axial tilt, rotation period, magnetic field, and crust thickness for the earth are exactly in balance to create conditions conducive for life.
- The atmosphere's oxygen/nitrogen ratio, carbon dioxide, water vapor and ozone levels are just right for life.
- If the moon was closer to the earth, tides would be greatly increased. High tide waves could sweep across the continents. The seas themselves might heat to the boiling point from the resulting friction. On the other hand, a more distant moon would reduce the tides. Marine life would be endangered by stagnant water!

It appears that the earth's "place in space" is just right for us.

[1] - https://answersingenesis.org/evidence-for-creation/the-universe-is-finely-tuned-for-life/

AGE OF THE EARTH

Now we'll move in from the universe to examine the apparent age of the earth we live on. Again, the expectations provided by the two models are very different:

Creationist Expectation	Evolutionist Expectation
The earth was created within the last 6,000 to 10,000 years according to the genealogies traced in the Bible.	**The earth is several billion years old.** The theory of evolution requires millions of years for changes to take place.

Evidence

Written History

The most reliable evidence available is the written history of men. The oldest records (other than the Bible) go back to about 3000 B.C. in Egypt and Babylon. Prior to that there is no known written history. Therefore science (which is based on human observation) can only speculate (guess) about anything prior to approximately 5000 years ago.

Aging Measurements and Methods

The various methods men have used to guess the age of the earth are based upon natural processes we observe today. Each method basically consists of:

- measuring the current state of a physical system and then
- measuring its rate of change.

This change is normally an exponential rate of decay expressed as a "half-life" of a certain duration. The half life is then used to calculate how long the system should have been in existence to reach its current state.

43

This seems like a logical approach, and there are several processes that are worldwide and capable of being measured. However, there are some assumptions that are being made:

1. **Constant rate** - It is assumed that the system has always changed at the same rate as found today.
2. **Closed system** - It is assumed that the system is a closed system, which means there are no external influences.
3. **Initial state** - It is assumed that we know what the initial condition of the system was when it came into being.

These are obviously very bold assumptions, and if any one of them is not valid the aging measurement from the process could be totally inaccurate.

Let's look at an analogy. Let's say we have a pickup truck loaded with apples. Some of the apples are rotten and some are good. Now we want to determine how long the apples have been in the truck. We observe that 40% of the apples are rotten and that approximately 5% turned rotten today. So we divide 40% by 5% and determine that the apples have been in the truck for 8 days. Right?

Not necessarily. Let's examine the assumptions:
1. Constant rate? – How do we know that the rate of rottenness has been 5% since the beginning? What if there were no rotten apples for two weeks, then 20% turned rotten in a single day, then 10% the next day, none the next day, 5% the next day, and 5% today?
2. Closed system? – What if the weather had been cold for two months with no apples getting rotten, then it got hot for a week? What if the truck was recently moved from the shade to the sun? What if someone recently threw some rotten apples onto the truck, and these have caused the others to turn rotten at a much faster rate?

3.   Initial state? – How do we know that all the apples were good when the truck was loaded? What if 5% of them were already rotten? What would that do to our estimate?

The assumptions you make with this type of aging measurement are obviously critical, so we need to be careful not to pretend we can "prove" anything with these measurements since we can't verify the assumptions.

Here are a few key measurements used today. My goal is not to argue about the technical details of these methods, but simply to use them as examples of why we need to recognize the limitations of measurements that depend on unverifiable assumptions:

- **Radiometric Decay Processes**
  These measurements compare the ratio of natural carbon to radiocarbon in organic material to determine how long it has been dead. These methods are sometimes accurate at dating events we can check in the last 3000 years, and they have been assumed to be accurate for much older results. If you make the three assumptions discussed above these methods can give ages in millions of years. But if you change the assumptions you can get very different results.

  Another problem with this method is that the rate of decay of carbon can be changed by electrical charges. This means that every electrical storm might change the dating of organic material.

- **Uranium Decay Processes**
  These processes are based on measuring the rate of decay from different types of uranium found within rocks into different types of lead. The two unverifiable assumptions in this method involve knowing the original ratio of uranium and lead in a rock and the assumption that no other changes have altered the ratio of uranium to lead.

The results given by these methods can indicate very old rock ages, even on rocks recently formed by volcanoes. These new rocks formed by volcanoes have both uranium and lead in them (initial state assumption is wrong), and thus this method can show that the rocks are very old even though they are not. This is not proof that the aging method is wrong, but it is another reason to question the assumptions.

- **Potassium-Argon Decay Process**
  This is another decay process used often by scientists because it consistently yields old rock ages. It makes the same assumptions as the other decay processes and has the same problems.

- **Growth of Total Human Population**
  A study of the mathematics of population indicates that two people plus a growth rate of 0.5 percent per year would have resulted in the current world's population in about 4000 years. The current growth rate is nearly 2.0 percent per year. Thus even factoring in wars and plagues it appears that people have only been around for a few thousand years. If people had been around for a million years, lived normal life times, and averaged 2.5 children per family (conservative until recent times) we would now have (10 to the 2700th power) people on earth. That's a ten with 2700 zeroes after it!

- **Others**
  There are many other processes (such as measuring the flow of chemicals and minerals into the ocean) that indicate ages of from 100 years to 500,000,000 years. They all can be attacked and defended by scientists, but neither the methods nor the assumptions they are based on can be proven.

What Does the Evidence Indicate?

We can sum up this evidence with the phrase **"CAN'T SAY"**. Some methods can be interpreted to support the Creation model, but some methods can also be interpreted to support the Evolution model **IF** the assumptions are correct. Since we can't verify the assumptions we'll be conservative and say that the evidence is not conclusively in favor of either model.

Creationist Interpretation

Much of this evidence can support the theory of a (relatively) young earth. Several measurements correspond very well with a reasonable Biblical time-frame. Since the earth was formed fully mature it's hard to even know what we should expect to find as evidence in the minerals of the earth.

Evolutionist Interpretation

Aging methods are probably the strongest argument for evolution. However, evolutionists are very selective in accepting the validity of these methods[1]. The methods usually referred to by "mainstream scientists" point to a much older earth, but these methods are also the most uncertain as far as the assumptions of rate/closed/state. Methods that show a more recent beginning also have strong points in their favor, yet evolutionists refer only to those that result in millions of years. The fact that several solid pieces of evidence point to a much younger earth does not shake their faith in the evolutionary time-frame, just as older earth evidence does not shake the faith of creationists. But it does confirm that we are talking about faith, not science.

[1] - http://christiananswers.net/q-aig/aig-c007.html

WHY SO IMPOSSIBLY LONG?

If the aging estimation methods are not conclusive, why do evolutionists insist on incredibly long periods of time? Is there a reason that their "bias" would require millions and billions of years?

Yes, there is. *I believe the major reason evolutionists are adamant about such incomprehensible periods of time is because.....they are incomprehensible!* None of us can really envision a time period of millions or billions of years. The 2000 years since Christ is a very long time for our minds, and there are 500 of those time periods in a million years. If scientists say that the earth is over 4 billion years old, that is 2,000,000 of the 2000-year periods of time since Christ. Our brains can't fathom that much time. So if someone says that something happened during a period of time that we can't even comprehend, how can we dispute it?

Evolutionary theory has no clear fossil evidence, no viable explanation for the origin of life, no reasonable mechanism for how new genetic information could have come about. So if someone said that evolution created our incredible complexity of life within a time period we could grasp, we would think that sounded ridiculous. *But with a time frame that is impossible to comprehend, the impossible seems more possible.*

LIFE FROM NON-LIVING MATTER

This is a critical question. Where did life come from? Some evolutionists will argue that this is not part of the theory of evolution, but I think that evolution at least strongly implies that there is a natural explanation for the origin of life. Here are the expectations:

Creationist Expectation	Evolutionist Expectation
1. **Life was supernaturally created by God**	1. **Life was created by an accident of nature**
2. **Life comes only from other life** and cannot spontaneously spring into being from non-living materials	2. **Life originally came from non-living matter** and under the right conditions could be formed from non-living matter today

Evidence

After massive efforts in scientific research there is still no known natural explanation for the formation of life. I'll leave the details to folks like Answers In Genesis and other creation scientists and organizations, but I'll give a few examples (you can skip to the last one if you're not interested in the details):

- All observations about living creatures support the idea that *life only comes from other life*. No one has ever observed life coming into existence from non-living matter.
- *Science has not succeeded in creating life from non-living matter even under unnatural conditions.* Many years, dollars, and brilliant minds have been expended in this pursuit under the most ideal laboratory conditions, but these efforts have all failed. The ones still currently mentioned in textbooks (such as the Stanley Miller experiment to create amino acids in 1953) are no longer considered viable

explanations by scientists, but no one has removed them from public "references".

- *(Warning – this is a little technical)*
  The formation of a living system from non-living matter is statistically in the realm of "impossible". Life is incredibly complex. The following steps would be necessary for the chemical production of a first living cell:

  a. Random atoms must be formed into amino acids
  b. These amino acids must link together to form chains (polypeptides)
  c. These chains must become long (hundreds of amino acids) and they must form in an ordered sequence, since there are 20 kinds of amino acids. This produces a simple protein molecule.
  d. More complex proteins must be produced.
  e. Very long and highly ordered molecular chains known as DNA must be formed and maintained
  f. An enormously complex chemical factory must be produced, complete with special protein formations, enzymes, DNA, RNA, ribosomes, a cell wall, etc. This single cell must be able to reproduce itself and carry on all the functions of life.

  To examine the odds that these steps occurred let's generously assume an ideal environment with amino acids already formed, catalysts, and the right temperature and moisture:
  - Walter Bradley, PhD, materials science, and Charles Thaxton, PhD, chemistry, calculated that the probability of amino acids forming into a protein is: 4.9×10^{-191}. This is well beyond the laws of probability (1×10^{-50}), and a protein is not even close to becoming a complete living cell.

- All living proteins are built of amino acids that are exclusively "left-handed" in their molecular orientation. The chances of forming left or right handed amino acids are about the same, so the odds that a chain of 400 left-handed-only amino acids would form is the same as the odds of flipping a coin and getting tails 400 times in a row. This is a probability of 1 in 10 to the 120th power (a 10 followed by 120 zeroes). This would form **one** protein molecule, and hundreds of such molecules would be needed in the first living system.
- The amino acids in the above example must be linked in a meaningful sequence. There are 20 kinds of amino acids and they must be linked in particular sequences.
- A cell contains a chain of about three billion pairs of molecules, and the sequence of these molecules is crucial. The odds of this happening by chance are essentially zero.
- It is estimated that the amount of time required to form even one gene by chance might be compared to the amount of time it would take to wear away a stone the size of the solar system if one atom was removed every billion years!

Sir Fred Hoyle, PhD, astronomy, and Chandra Wickramasinghe, professor of applied math and astronomy, calculated that the odds of amino acids forming together in the proper sequence for life was 1 in 10 to the 40,000th power. All of these statistics point to a probability of zero.

If this is not enough, there is also the fact that every chemical reaction along the way is reversible. A molecule that came together by chance is unstable and could easily break back down.

- If the above examples were a little complicated, this last one is pretty simple. ***One of the best evidences that there is no*** *viable natural explanation for the origin of life is the testimony of the evolutionists themselves.* When some of the most well-known evolutionists such as Richard Dawkins and Isaac Asimov state that perhaps life was brought to earth from other planets, you know they recognize the lack of any natural explanation. They are grasping at any straw that allows them to deny that life requires a supernatural Creator.

What Does the Evidence Indicate?

As far as the development of life from non-living matter, the answer from the evidence is very clear: **"NO WAY"**.

Creationist Interpretation

A creationist would say that all of this is simply proof that God created life by purposeful design. We cannot even come up with another feasible theory, so certainly there is nothing "blind" about having faith in the Bible's account of the origin of life.

Evolutionist Interpretation

Evolutionary scientists have clearly taken a leap of faith when they assert that life began from non-living chemicals. The origin of the first life form is just assumed to be an accident of nature because the most obvious alternative explanation is God. Evolutionists find it easier to accept the miracle of a statistically impossible event than to accept a miracle from God.

COMPLEX ANIMALS FROM SIMPLE LIFE

A commonly accepted premise (which comes from evolution) is that simpler creatures eventually "evolve" into more complex ones. So we can look at the evidence and see if it supports the idea that the creatures we see today are "self-improved" versions of their ancestors.

Creationist Expectation	Evolutionist Expectation
1. **Each type of animal / creature was initially created in its full complexity** and all were created at the same time. 2. **There are no transitional forms** where one kind turned into another because all kinds were created fully formed and God made each "after his own kind" (Genesis 1:24,25)	1. **Each complex creature evolved from a less complex creature** 2. **There should be transitional forms** of animals which show the change from one kind into another. 3. Creatures originated in the sea, evolved into land creatures, and then evolved into flying creatures.

Evidence

Genetic Information

Scientists have made progress in understanding the genetic code that is the blueprint for life. The results show that the information coded into life is incredibly complex. Our genes comprise a sophisticated information processing system which far exceeds the abilities of our best computing technology. Here are some facts from the article "DNA – The Language of Life" on the Answers in Genesis web site:

- A single strand of DNA is thousands of times thinner than a strand of human hair.

- One pinhead of DNA could hold enough information to fill a stack of books stretching from the earth to the moon 500 times.
- Though DNA is wound into tight coils, cells can quickly access, copy, and translate the information stored in DNA.
- DNA even has a built-in proofreader and spell-checker that ensures precise copying. Only about one mistake slips through for every 10 billion nucleotides that are copied.
- All of the information for each cell in a creature is stored and processed and passed along to offspring.

The big question is…. where did the information and its system come from?

Evolution claims that mutations (errors) in the transfer of genetic information are the source of new species and increasing complexity. Evolutionists claim that mutations cause new physical characteristics, then natural selection singles out the mutations that are beneficial and preserves them in succeeding generations.

Is this a reasonable theory? Is natural selection "smart" enough to preserve beneficial new information? Could mutations explain where the information comes from?

Here are just a few of the problems with evolution's assumptions about mutations:

- **Mutations most often result in a *loss* of useful information**. The likelihood of any mutation being beneficial is very remote. Normal genes require not only information, but also a function that uses the information and a mechanism for transferring that information to succeeding generations. *Nearly all of the permanent genetic changes we observe involve a loss of some information that was already there.* Our observation is that we're actually losing information rather than gaining it!
  - For example, a harmful bacterium becomes resistant to antibiotics because it <u>loses</u> a genetic characteristic that

allowed the antibiotic to affect it. This doesn't explain how the characteristic got there in the first place.

- **"Molecules to man" evolution requires a statistically impossible amount of new genetic information to be added**. The amount of information that would have to be added to turn a single-cell microscopic bacterium (which already has an estimated 1 trillion bits of DNA information) into a giraffe is beyond comprehension. Mutations alone could not originate and retain the information needed to turn a single-cell creature into a complex creature.

- **A mutation would have to result in a fully-operational function in order to be "beneficial"**. The theory is that natural selection would "choose" a mutation when it gave the creature a benefit over creatures without the mutation. But, for example, a single mutation to the genetic information for a reptile could not add all the information needed to suddenly give the creature a fully functioning wing. A non-functional or partial wing would be a disadvantage that would not survive in nature.

And consider an incredible wonder such as a caterpillar that has the ability to spin a cocoon around itself, metamorphose and grow wings, then emerge and become a butterfly that can lay eggs to hatch out more caterpillars! *How could gradual small mutations allow a creature to survive while "evolving" such abilities?*

So what we see in the fields of genetics and information technology is:

There is no known natural source for the incredible amount of genetic information that exists.

INSTINCT

One related topic that I find fascinating is the existence of what we call instinct. This is the innate ability of a creature to know how to do something that it has never done before.

- How does a baby know how to suckle as soon as it is born, and how does a new mother know how to "mother"?
- How does a bird or butterfly know how to navigate hundreds or thousands of miles to a place it has never been before?
- How does a hen know to break up food for her chicks when she's never done it before?
- How do salmon know how to return upstream to spawn?
- How does any creature know how to do something that it hasn't been "taught"?

There are thousands of amazing unlearned behaviors that we see in animals. In my opinion, **scientists use the term "instinct" to mean** *"We don't have any idea how this creature knows how to do that, so we'll call it instinct."*

Instinct is a very powerful evidence for a Designer. He gave creatures instinct so they would know how to do things without the need to learn them via experience. Some creatures have short life cycles and don't have much time to "learn", so without instinct they wouldn't survive.

How does that innate knowledge get there? Can it be explained by random mutations over millions of years? It takes a lot more faith to believe that instinct happened by accident than it does to believe God gave it to His creatures.

Fossil Record

The fossil record has an abundance of evidence from the past. Darwin thought that over time more fossils would be found that confirm his theory. Hundreds of thousands of fossilized life forms have been found all over the world since Darwin's time, and they clearly proclaim ......*that Darwin was wrong.* No living creature has been found that exhibits the characteristics of a transitional form. Within a kind there are variations, but always within the kind. The adaptive ability of animals is always exhibited without changing the basic nature or kind of the animal.

The book <u>Evolution - The Challenge of the Fossil Record</u> by Dr. Duane Gish covers the details of this very well, so I will just present a summary of some highlights:

1. **Complex creatures from the beginning** - The oldest fossil record shows simple single-celled organisms alongside fully formed complex animals such as jellyfish, sea urchins, worms, sponges, and trilobites. The complex animals are just suddenly there in the fossil record - there are no fossils of any transitional forms linking the single-celled with the complex animals.
2. **Insects haven't changed** - The fossils of insects bear an amazing resemblance to living insects today. There are also no transitional forms showing, say, a non-flying insect evolving into a flying insect.
3. **No transition to skeletons** - No fossil evidence can be found to show that an invertebrate animal (without a skeletal structure) evolved into a vertebrate. The physiological differences between vertebrates and invertebrates are significant, so this should have required a long evolutionary process. However, no transitional fossils have been found.
4. **No fish switching to land** - No transitional fossils can be found which show any form of fish changing into a land

animal. There is no fossil evidence showing a fin turning into a foot.

5. **No obvious intermediate forms** - There are claims of transitional fossils between amphibians, reptiles, and mammals. Most of the difference between living animals in these classes is found in the soft parts of their bodies, not the hard parts subject to fossilization. Yet even evolutionists admit that there are no transitional forms showing a complete evolutionary sequence for any of the thirty-two orders of mammals.(Gish pg. 78)

6. **No transition to flight** - There is no fossil evidence of transitional forms between non-flying and flying animals. This should have taken millions of years according to evolutionists. Yet there are no fossils showing this transition. As Dr. Gary Parker humorously points out in one of our favorite recorded messages, a land creature trying to transition to flying would have a tough time surviving the interim phases!

7. **No "half-dinosaurs"** - The fossil record of dinosaurs is one of the most widely publicized. These creatures apparently existed, but there are no fossils which show a common ancestry with any other creature. There are also no transitional fossils indicating that any dinosaur ever turned into anything else.

Each kind of creature first appears in the fossil record as a fully-formed, fully-functioning creature. ***There is no fossil evidence of one kind developing from another kind.***

What Does the Evidence Indicate?

If we're looking for evidence that simple life evolved into more complex life or that one type of life changed into another, we'd have to say that the evidence **"LACKS GENES and 'TWEENS"** for any natural explanation:

- **LACKS GENES** - There is no viable source of the genetic information.
- **LACKS 'TWEENS** – There is no real supporting record of intermediate fossils, of something "in between" two kinds.

Creationist Interpretation

The genetic evidence is consistent with the idea that the incredible complexity of life required intelligent design. The fossil record certainly seems to agree with the theory that God created each kind of animal to remain "after his own kind." At least this theory fits the known facts. The only problem is the supposed age of these fossils (millions of years), and we've already discussed the shaky assumptions of the aging methods.

Evolutionist Interpretation

The information and genetic evidence is a huge hurdle for evolution to overcome, so many evolutionists seem to stay away from this area. The fossil record is a cornerstone of the supposed evidence for evolution, and the evolutionist insists that there were transitional forms - if he didn't believe that he would have to give up on evolution! The evolutionist will sometimes point to environmental adaptation as evidence of evolution, but this has never crossed species lines. Again, the evolutionist must have faith in spite of the evidence, not because of it.

Some evolutionists have even proposed the idea that evolution works in "rapid bursts" (punctuated equilibrium model) which explains the lack of transitional fossils. But what's the suggested proof for this theory? *The complete lack of transitional fossils!*

MAN FROM ANIMALS

One of the standard ideas taught in public schools is that men evolved from apes or that men and apes had a common ancestor.

Creationist Expectation	Evolutionist Expectation
1. **Man was created fully formed by God.** 2. **Man should appear in the fossil record at the same time as other life forms,** although not in the same abundance. There were fewer men and they lived longer at first. 3. There should be **no evidence of man "evolving"** from any other type of animal.	1. **Man is simply another complex animal** which evolved from less complex animals. 2. There should be many **millions of years of fossil record before man appears** in the record. 3. There should be **evidence of transitional forms** linking man to earlier similar animals.

Evidence

Evolutionists assume that evolution is an ongoing process. *There is no evidence today that man is changing into another species.*

The genetic/information evidence for man is the same as for simple to complex creatures in the previous section. *There is no known natural source for the genetic information found in humans.* Even the reports proclaiming the similarity of human DNA with chimpanzee DNA is simply another fact that is interpreted based on bias. A creationist sees "same Designer" while an evolutionist sees "same ancestor". An evolutionist's claim that there is "only a 4% DNA difference between chimps and humans" *would still represent over 40 million distinct mutations since the "common ancestor",* a number way too large for even the evolutionary timeframe.

Gish's book again does an excellent job of outlining the human fossil evidence from the past. *There is no real evidence that man has ever been anything but a man.* Here is a summary:

1. There are no transitional fossils linking the so-called Primate order (which includes monkeys, apes, and men) with any non-Primates. Primates just suddenly appear in the fossil record.
2. There are no transitional fossils which link the "primitive" primates such as lemurs with other primates.
3. There have been only a few supposed primate transitional forms found in the fossil record. Some have been shown to be frauds. Some have been identified as apes after closer examination. Some have been identified as men after closer examination. The major indication that any of these forms is a "link" is the supposed age of the fossils. The aging techniques have problems which were discussed earlier. In fact, some of the fossil discoveries later found evidence of man in rock layers **underneath** the supposed ancestors of man.

Examples:
- Nebraska man – turned out to be a pig's tooth
- Piltdown man – turned out to be a hoax
- Peking man - the fossils were lost before they were examined by objective scientists
- Java man - turned out to be a combination of bones from a man and a gibbon (monkey)
- Neanderthal man - a man with rickets
- Cro Magnon man - simply a very intelligent man
- "Lucy" - almost identical to the modern pygmy chimpanzee

What Does the Evidence Indicate?

The conclusion here is the same as for complex animals from simple – **"LACKS GENES and TWEENS"**.

Creationist Interpretation

Nothing in the fossil record indicates that it is "unscientific" to believe in God's special creation of man.

Evolutionist Interpretation

Evolutionists again believe in the evolution of man despite no clear supporting evidence. There is no evidence in the present or the past that man has ever been anything but man. However, since creation is unacceptable to men who reject the idea of God, evolutionists simply believe that man evolved without leaving any fossil traces of the steps of the transformation (Gish pg 222). It certainly seems to be a stretch to call this a scientific theory!

SUMMARY OF THE INSPECTION

Here is an easily-memorized summary of what we found in the evidence:

- Nature of the Universe - **DECAY**
- Age of the Earth - **CAN'T SAY**
- Life from Non-Life - **NO WAY**
- Animals and Man from simpler life forms - **LACKS GENES AND 'TWEENS**

N - No Compromise

Is it possible to believe that both the Bible <u>and</u> evolution are true? Could God have used evolution to "create"? Many sincere Christians have tried to find a way to reconcile what the Bible teaches about our origins with current scientific theories. *However, closer examination shows that you must either believe the Bible accounts as they are given or reject the authority of the Bible.* Reinterpreting or ignoring the plain meaning of the Bible is the same as rejecting its authority.

The following acrostic "DON'T" summarizes four key reasons a Christian cannot logically reconcile the biblical account of our origins with any of the evolution-based compromise positions:

- **D**eath did not come before mankind and sin
- **O**rder of creation is not consistent with evolution
- **N**ames in genealogies do not allow for evolutionary timeframe
- **T**en Commandments point to seven-day creation week as a model for our week

COMPROMISE THEORIES

Many have tried to reconcile Genesis with evolution by "interpreting" Genesis 1 - 11 in ways such as the following theories::

Day-Age Theory

> This interpretation says that the days in Genesis were not 24 hour days, but were instead the geological ages taught by evolution. The Hebrew word used for "day" ("yom") may refer to an ordinary 24-hour day, or it may be used to mean an indefinite period of time (such as "the day of the Lord"). It cannot mean a definite LONG period. You have to read it in context to determine which meaning is intended. The author says "and there was evening, and there was morning" on each day. A plain reading of this wording clearly settles that the author intended to describe a literal 24 hour day.

> The passage in 2 Peter 3:8 that compares a day to a thousand years is sometimes used to defend this theory. That passage is not defining "day" as a thousand years. In context the passage has nothing to do with creation, but is poetically describing the fact that God is outside of time and is not limited by it.

> The sequence of the account in creation also has no relation to the theoretical geological ages (see "Order of Creation" below) - God created large animals before small animals and insects! This theory also implies that the death shown in the fossil record existed before the fall of man, which is totally contradictory to the doctrine of the Bible (see "Death" below).

The Pre-Adamic Gap Theory

This theory says that between Genesis 1:1 and 1:2 there were 5 billion years of geologic/fossil history before Satan's fall caused a worldwide cataclysm that left the earth "without form and void." Again, there is no evidence for this in the Bible and this theory requires that man, death, and suffering existed before the Creation/Fall account of Genesis.

The Genealogical-Gap Theory

This theory attempts to reconcile the Bible to evolution by proposing that there are gaps of at least a million years in the genealogies given in Genesis. Since the genealogies are also recorded in 1 Chronicles and Luke we must assume that they were meant to be taken as essentially complete records of the line from Adam through Noah to Abraham to Jesus.

WHY COMPROMISE IS NOT VALID

<u>D</u>   Death
According to Scripture, death entered the world through Adam.

- *"Therefore, just as sin entered the world through one man, and death through sin, and in this way death came to all men, because all sinned"* (Romans 5:12)
- *"For since death came through a man, the resurrection of the dead comes also through a man. For as in Adam all die, so in Christ all will be made alive."* (1 Corinthians 15:21-22).

Evolutionary-based theories insist that death is one of the building blocks that "created" life as we know it now. As a Christian, to accept evolution you would have to reject the Bible's clear teaching about death and insist that death existed long before Adam. ***The Bible teaches that death came after man, which is totally incompatible with the concept of evolution.***

<u>O</u>   Order of Creation
According to Genesis 1, the sequence of creation is not compatible with the evolutionary sequence of origins. These can't be reconciled with a "long day" or any other attempts to rationalize that the Bible and evolution are compatible.

The Bible says that God created the world and universe in a totally different sequence than evolution would require.

Genesis 1 Sequence	Evolution Sequence
First life was on land (Gen 1:11)	First life was in primeval oceans
Earth before sun and moon and stars (Gen 1:14-19)	Sun and moon at least as old as earth
Stars after earth (Gen 1:16)	Stars before earth
Light over the earth before sun, moon, and stars (Gen 1:3)	Earth's light from sun and stars
Earth created covered with water	Earth first formed as molten blob
Plant life before sun and stars	Plant life after sunlight
Birds before insects	Insects before birds
Birds and fish created at same time	Fish evolved millions of years before birds
First animal was largest - whales! (Gen 1:21)	Long evolution from smallest organisms
Plants before insects	Insect pollination required for plants
Death came after man sinned	Death occurred millions of years before man

There are dozens of these discrepancies in the sequence. No amount of clever suggestions about how long it took for God to create can address this irreconcilable difference.

N   Names

In Genesis chapters 5 and 11 there are genealogies that run from the time of Adam through Abraham. These are obviously written very precisely to document the exact number of years of each generation. These names would not be meaningful unless the writer intended them to be literal. Those who contend that a "day" could be a million years need to consider these two facts:

- Adam was created on day six.
- Adam lived through day six, and day seven, and died when he was 930 years old

The charts below illustrate how much the lives of these early generations overlapped (Adam lived for 153 years after Methuselah was born!). When we combine the fact that Adam was created "very good" (genetically perfect) with the fact that these men lived a long time alongside the men of previous generations, it is easy to understand how mankind achieved cities, metalworking, music, and other advancements within the first few generations.

The Bible details how long the key men lived in the first generations after Creation, and this is totally inconsistent with the millions of years that evolution says were required to create man.

Interesting Points to Note on the Charts:

- Notice how quickly the life spans decreased after the flood

- Some people believe that Methuselah's name means "when he dies, it shall be sent." Methuselah died the same year the Flood happened (1656 After Creation). Some even suggest that Methuselah's godly father, Enoch, may have been given a prophecy by God that led to that name. If so, the fact that Methuselah had the longest recorded life is a sign of God's long-suffering patience during the time of Noah (1 Peter 3:20).

- Adam was still alive until Noah's father Lamech was 56 years old.

- Noah died just 2 years before Abraham was born.

- Shem was still alive during the life of Abraham. Abraham could have spoken to Shem (Noah's son), who probably knew his great-grandfather Methuselah, who in turn could have spoken to Adam, the first man.

- Abraham was 150 years old before Shem died.

Genesis Genealogies (A.C. is After Creation)			
Name	**Born**	**Died**	**Life Span**
Adam	0 A.C. (Day 6)	930 A.C.	930 years
Seth	130 A.C.	1042 A.C.	912 years
Enosh	235 A.C.	1140 A.C.	905 years
Kenan	325 A.C.	1235 A.C.	910 years
Mahalalel	395 A.C.	1290 A.C.	895 years
Jared	460 A.C.	1422 A.C.	962 years
Enoch	622 A.C.	(*God took him away in 987 A.C.)	365* years
Methuselah	687 A.C.	1656 A.C.	969 years
Lamech	874 A.C.	1651 A.C.	777 years
Noah	1056 A.C.	2006 A.C.	950 years
Flood came in 1656 A.C.			
Shem	1558 A.C.	2158 A.C.	600 years
Arphaxad	1658 A.C.	2096 A.C.	438 years
Shelah	1693 A.C.	2126 A.C.	433 years
Eber	1723 A.C.	2187 A.C.	464 years
Peleg	1757 A.C.	1996 A.C.	239 years
Reu	1787 A.C.	2026 A.C.	239 years
Serug	1819 A.C.	2049 A.C.	230 years
Nahor	1849 A.C.	1997 A.C.	148 years
Terah	1878 A.C.	2083 A.C.	205 years
Abram (Abraham)	2008 A.C.	2183 A.C.	175 years

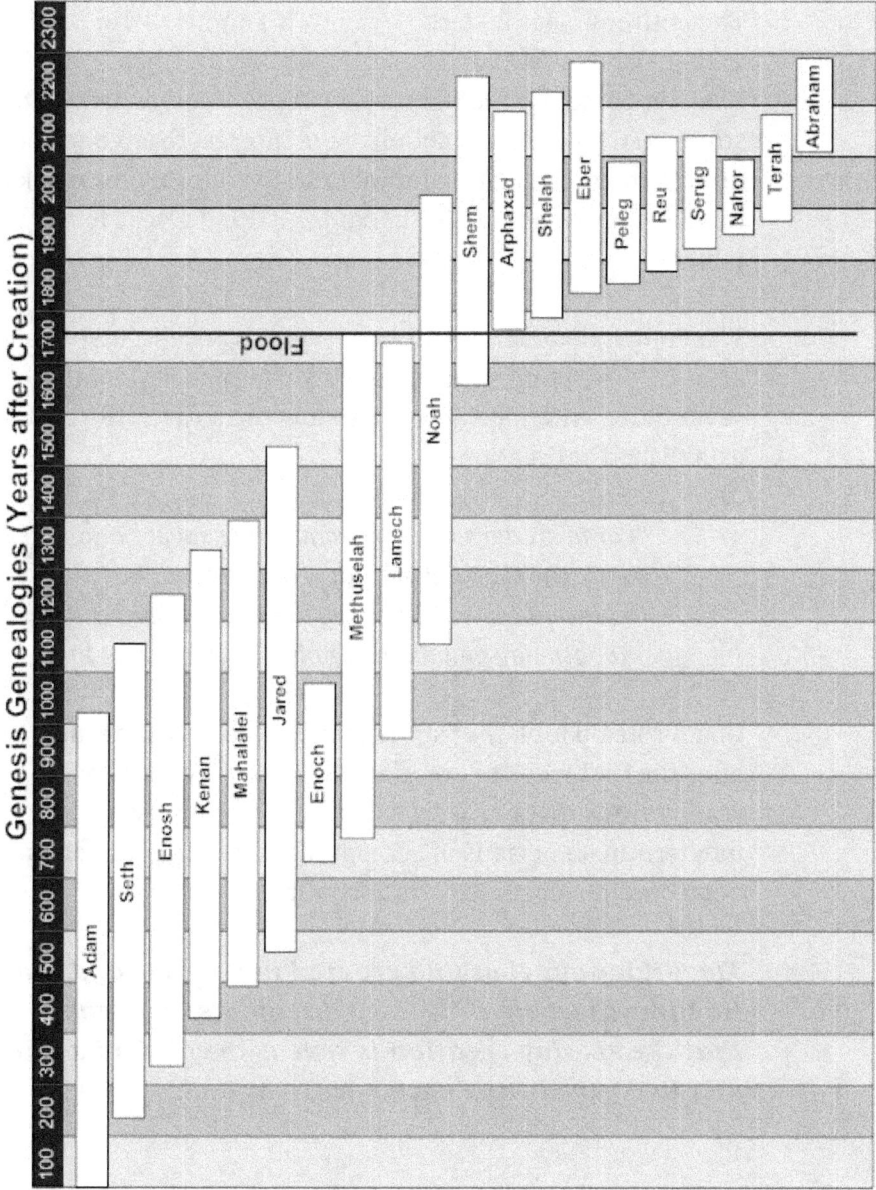

Genesis Genealogies (Years after Creation)

<u>T</u>   ## Ten Commandments

The entire Bible is inspired by God (2 Timothy 3:16, 2 Peter 1:20-21), but a few verses are physically <u>inscribed</u> by God. The Ten Commandments were written by God on tablets of stone, so they certainly should be of interest to anyone who desires to know what God thinks. In Exodus 20 God speaks the Ten Commandments. In Exodus 31 God gives Moses the tablets.

The Fourth Commandment is relevant to our discussion of origins. When God says to work six days and rest on the seventh He says that we are to follow the pattern He established at Creation.

> *"For in six days the Lord made the heavens and the earth, the sea, and all that is in them, but he rested on the seventh day. Therefore the Lord blessed the Sabbath day and made it holy."* (Exodus 20:11).

God wrote on tablets of stone that our week is patterned after the first week of Creation. For us to say that God really means that our week is patterned after seven indeterminate periods of geologic ages is ludicrous and is not a credible position from Scripture.

The Bible says that God created in six days and that He Himself wrote this down on tablets. To deny that the six-day creation is true is to call God a liar and to discredit the entire Word of God.

EMBARRASSED BY THE SUPERNATURAL?

Nearly everyone agrees that a plain reading of the Genesis 1 account results in an understanding that God created everything in six days. So why do so many who claim to follow Jesus reject this understanding? Why are so many compromise theories proposed by people within the church?

It seems that the motive for compromise results from a desire to fit millions of years into the biblical account. Because popular opinion has accepted millions of years as "scientific", a supernatural six-day creation is embarrassing to many Christians. So they treat the creation account as a fable that is not really worth defending. After all, it doesn't matter what people think about creation as long as they believe the Gospel and trust in Christ, right?

IT DOES MATTER! The Virgin birth is supernatural. The miracles of Christ are supernatural. The Holy Spirit is supernatural. And the resurrection of Christ is supernatural. Is it more difficult to believe that God created as He said than to believe that God became man and rose from the dead? These truths MUST be supernatural or there is no gospel and Christians are to be pitied (1 Cor 15:12-19).

We damage our credibility as Christ's ambassadors when we deny a supernatural creation and then try to present a supernatural gospel of Jesus Christ.

So if you are tempted to take a compromise position that denies a literal six-day creation in which God spoke everything into existence out of nothing, just remember: **DON'T**.

JESUS, THE IMAGINATIVE CREATOR AND SUSTAINER

For by him all things were created: things in heaven and on earth, visible and invisible, whether thrones or powers or rulers or authorities; all things were created by him and for him. He is before all things, and in him all things hold together. Colossians 1:16-17

Not only is there strong evidence for God as Creator, but creation shouts for recognition of His infinite imagination. He didn't have to create variety and beauty in order to have a functional creation. A mindless, accidental universe would not likely produce much color or variety. But Jesus did: Jesus, with **unlimited imagination, unlimited power, and unlimited resources** created a world that reflects the glory and nature of God. Every unique bug, butterfly, sunset, bird, pebble, mountain, flower, vegetable, and person is a testament to His imagination. And as part of that creation He gave us senses so that we can enjoy and explore it forever. What a gift!

The passage above also says that "in him all things hold together." It's a sobering and humbling thought to realize that all the forces that hold our bodies and universe together (atoms, molecules, gravity, etc.) **are sustained each moment by Jesus**. Science recognizes these forces, but doesn't have an explanation for them. If Jesus stopped holding things together, that would be the end of us. What a blessing that we can trust that He is able and willing to sustain all that He created, and that those He saves will be able to delight in His imagination and provision forever.

ORIGIN Recap

When we ask the question "where did we come from" the answer is a matter of ORIGIN:

Only Two Choices

> Either God created us as He said, or we don't know how we got here because there were no witnesses.

Realize the Significance

> The origin of everything is a matter of deep importance. If God created as He said, He owns us and has the right to say what is right and what is wrong. If He didn't create as He said, no one owns us and no one has the right to say what is right or wrong. And if we don't trust His Word about our origins, why should we trust the rest of the Bible?

Is it Faith or Science?

> The one-time origin of the universe/world/life/etc. is not a subject for science. Science is for the study of theories that meet the LAB requirements:
>
> > **L**ookable - you can see it happening
> > **A**ccessible - you can go to it or bring it to you for study
> > **B**reakable - you can devise a test that would disprove the theory
>
> Neither of the theories of special creation or of evolution meet these criteria, so the question of origin is a matter of belief and faith.

Guess at the Evidence

> Although we can't use science to prove or disprove our beliefs about origin, we can use it to investigate whether our belief is consistent with the evidence we see. We can speculate about what we would <u>expect</u> to observe in the universe around us if our belief was true, then we can see if the evidence matches our expectations. Creation and

evolutionary beliefs result in very different assumptions about:
-       The properties of the universe
-       The age of the earth
-       The origin of life
-       The origin of different species of life
-       The origin of man

Inspect the Evidence

When we look at the evidence we see the following results:
-       Universe - "Decay"
-       Age of the earth - "Can't say"
-       Origin of life by natural means - "No way"
-       Origin of species and man by evolution - "Lacks Genes and 'Tweens'"

No Compromise

All of the evidence in Scripture says "DON'T compromise with evolutionary thinking"
- **D**eath did not come before mankind and sin
- **O**rder of creation is not consistent with evolution
- **N**ames in genealogies do not allow for evolutionary timeframe
- **T**en Commandments point to seven-day creation week as a model for our week

REVIEW

We are all biased - Our answers to life's big questions are based 99.99% on our bias, our assumptions about the "whole ball" that we don't know first-hand.

- If there is Someone who knows the whole ball it is logical to get our answers from Him.
- If there is no one who knows it all we have to rely on our reason, which would be the result of random, purposeless accidents.

Beginnings - ORIGIN

- **O**nly Two Choices
- **R**ealize the Significance
- **I**s it Faith or Science?
    - o   LAB - **L**ookable, **A**ccessible, **B**reakable
- **G**uess at the Evidence
- **I**nspect the Evidence
    - o   Universe = **"Decay"**
    - o   Age of the Earth = **"Can't Say"**
    - o   Origin of Life by Chance = **"No Way"**
    - o   Evolution of Species and Man = **"Lacks Genes and Tweens"**
- **N**o Compromise - DON'T
    - o   **D**eath after man, not before
    - o   **O**rder of Creation
    - o   **N**ames in genealogies define timeframe
    - o   **T**en Commandments refer to seven-day week
    - o   **S**upernatural must be accepted for the gospel

.....still to come...
Intent of Life
Authority
Standards

2. WHY ARE WE HERE?
<u>I</u>ntent - The Purpose of L.I.F.E.

Our second big question asks if there is a reason for our being here. Obviously our answer to the first question (where did we come from?) has a lot to do with our answer to the second:

- If we were created <u>on</u> purpose then we must have <u>a</u> purpose.
- If we are here by accident then logically there can't be a real reason for our lives.

If we are here by chance.......
The origin of much of philosophy is rooted in this "intellectual" dilemma. Let's say we are secular humanists who reject the Creator and believe that man's thinking is the highest level of consciousness. This usually goes hand in hand with naturalism and materialism, the idea that everything is the result of natural materialistic processes and that there is no supernatural realm. We're feeling pretty good about ourselves at first because we can be our own masters without any accountability to a higher power. We're optimistic that our well-intentioned intellects will eventually solve all of mankind's problems if we can just root superstition out of people's thinking. Sure, there are problems in the world, but if we can keep from blowing ourselves up for a few more years then we're smart enough to figure out how to solve all those problems.

But wait! Just as we're starting to get excited about the self-exalting vision we've built for ourselves, we realize it doesn't have a foundation. If we are the product of natural evolution, then our prized consciousness is the product of random mutations! How can we trust our thinking? Could our thinking be wrong? Oh no, how could there even be a "wrong" thinking if all thinking is the product of chance?

Honest reflection on the thought that we are nothing but "random accidents" can lead to despair. Existentialism, hedonism, fatalism, and a variety of other "isms" are the logical destination of someone who tries to find a meaning<u>ful</u> end from a meaning<u>less</u> beginning. As secular humanists we could have "goals" for our lives that we could try to substitute for a purpose, but *we can't give real meaning to our lives if we are simply the product of millions of random events and accidents.* Just as with the concept of absolute right and wrong, if there is no purpose to our beginning we can't insist upon any real significance to the middle or end of our existence.

But, if we were put here for a purpose.......
If the God who created everything out of His own imagination created us for a purpose, then our life is meaningful. Even if we don't know why! We should try to figure out the why, but at the very least we know there <u>is</u> an answer. No one truly enjoys living without a purpose, and it is comforting to know that there is Someone who cares enough to have created us.

There is only one big downside to the idea of life having a true purpose:

If my life has true meaning, it also means that Someone Else is in charge of my life.

This is a stumbling point for our pride. Satan tempted Adam and Eve with the lie "you can be like God" and we continue to fall for this inviting fruit. I like being self-centered and setting my own course through life..... as long as things are going well. I'm like a little dog who likes to run ahead of my Master and act like I'm leading the way. But when I run into a bigger dog like trials and storms and sickness and tragedy and calamity and death I'm quick to tuck my tail and run back to the Master so He can take care of me.

So if we have a Master who made us for a reason, what's the reason? *Why does someone who has everything need me?*

According to the Bible, God made us for His own glory (Isaiah 43:7; 1 Corinthians 10:31). I've always felt a little uncomfortable with this thought because it makes God seem so self-serving. But then I think, if He didn't make us for *His* glory, for whose glory would he make us? Mine? Yours? Mother Nature's? We will glorify someone or something with our lives, and it is logical that life will be better and more enjoyable if we seek to bring glory to God rather than to ourselves. He made us, He says He loves us, and He knows us inside out. I've lived in my body all my life and I still don't have a clue how to consciously make my heart beat or my cells reproduce or my lungs take in oxygen. If the One who knows everything says I'm here for His glory I can't imagine why I would think I could come up with a better reason.

So if we're here for God's glory, what are we supposed to do?

Many books have already been written to try to answer this question, so we're obviously not going to come up with an exhaustive answer in the next few pages. But for our purposes we're looking for a "big picture" outline that we can memorize. We'll use the acrostic LIFE to summarize some major elements of God's purpose for us as we find it in the Bible:

- <u>L</u>ove
- <u>I</u>ncrease
- <u>F</u>aithfulness
- <u>E</u>ternity

Within these topics we can organize enough thoughts to keep us busy for the rest of our lives (and beyond).

IMPOSSIBLE INSTRUCTIONS?

The instructions and commands God gives us are more than difficult for us to do. They are <u>impossible</u> to do in our own strength. But God promises to enable us to do the things He commands us to do. He is the one who gives us the ability to live the life He calls us to.

*May God himself, the God of peace, sanctify you through and through. May your whole spirit, soul and body be kept blameless at the coming of our Lord Jesus Christ. The one who calls you is faithful and **he will do it.*** 1 Thessalonians 5:23-24

*Because he himself suffered when he was tempted, **he is able to help those who are being tempted.*** Hebrews 2:18

***His divine power has given us everything we need for life and godliness** through our knowledge of him who called us by his own glory and goodness.* 2 Peter 1:3

GOD'S WILL FOR MY LIFE?

Often people will talk about God's will for them when they are faced with big decisions like careers, college, marriage, etc. We certainly should seek God's wisdom and guidance, but sometimes I think the term "God's will" is not properly used. At times God may give individuals a clear long-term vision or show them a lifetime direction. But normally God doesn't lift the veil of the future and show us where he's going to take us. He gives us guidance in the smaller day-to-day decisions we make, and these add up to a lifetime of following Him.

G.K. Chesterton said that God's will for our life is like a path through the woods. The only time we have to find the path is when we've wandered off of it. The goal is to stay in God's will (on the path) and let Him control where the path goes.

What God does show us clearly is who He wants us to **be**. My ability to please God with my life is not dependent on my ability to decipher the mystery of His long-term plan for me. What is important is that I respond in a God-honoring way to whatever happens. The story of Job is a lesson in humbly accepting God's right to bring blessings or allow curses – *"The LORD gave and the LORD has taken away; may the name of the LORD be praised."* Job 2:21. See also 1 Thessalonians 4:3-7, 1 Peter 2:15.

Whether or not I always make perfect decisions, I can always know God's will for me because He tells me plainly in the following verse:

*Be joyful always; pray continually; give thanks in all circumstances, **for this is God's will for you in Christ Jesus**.* 1 Thessalonians 5:16-18

L - LOVE

When Jesus was asked to identify the greatest commandments from God, this is what he said:

"The most important one," answered Jesus, "is this: 'Hear, O Israel, the Lord our God, the Lord is one. Love the Lord your God with all your heart and with all your soul and with all your mind and with all your strength.' The second is this: 'Love your neighbor as yourself.' There is no commandment greater than these." (Mark 12:29-31)

Obviously this topic of love is very important to God. In our culture we tend to view love in emotional terms, but the Bible paints love in the context of obedience. Jesus said "Whoever has my commands and obeys them, he is the one who loves me." (John 14:21) Jesus didn't say we had to <u>feel</u> loving toward him, although it is natural for us to love him in return for the incredible sacrifice he has made and the abundant provision he continues to make for us. If love is simply an emotion, we can easily use the excuse of not being able to help how we feel. ***But if love is instead a commitment to doing what is right and in the best interest of another***, then we CHOOSE to love by choosing to obey God's instructions on what is right.

If Jesus says these are the greatest commandments, let's look at how we accomplish God's purpose in our lives by obeying in the areas of loving Him and others:

LOVING GOD

If we rely on our own intellect to figure out ways to love God, we are quickly forced to admit defeat. Let's consider just a few of the challenges:

- **God is infinite** *(Where do you find Him?)*

- **God is spirit** and we can't see him in a literal sense *(How do you give Him a hug?)*
- **God owns everything** *(What gift do you give to someone who truly has everything?)*
- **God is perfect** *(How long will He enjoy being around me?)*

Mercifully, God has not left us to figure out how to love him. As with the statement of Jesus above, God says that we love Him by doing what He requires of us. This involves having the **right perspective**, **right actions,** and **right beliefs** related to God. We'll use the acrostic "GOD" to summarize these key aspects of loving God that we should continually strive to follow:

G - Glory of God (right perspective)

The perspective we need in order to love God is that *we are to continually seek to give glory to God with our lives*. The Bible says that God is a jealous God and that He will not share His glory with anyone else. To love God means to do our best to see that He receives glory for who He is and what He has done. Men are always giving glory to something - the proper focus of all glory is God.

So <u>how</u> do we glorify God? Again, the best answer is always to do it the way God says to do it. Here are some guidelines from Scripture that specify ways we can bring glory to God:

- Grow in knowledge and depth of insight so that we may be able to discern what is best (Philippians 1:9-11)
- Encourage men to bow their knee at the name of Jesus and to confess that he is Lord (Philippians 2:10-11)
- Speak as one speaking the words of God and serve with the strength God provides (1 Peter 4:11)
- Live such good lives among the pagans that they may see our good deeds and glorify God when He comes (1 Peter 2:12)

- Shine before men that they may see our good deeds and praise God (Matthew 5:16)
- Ask Jesus for great things so that he may bring glory to the Father (John 14:13)
- Bear much fruit and show ourselves to be Christ's disciples (John 15:8)
- Promote unity among believers so that with one heart and mouth we may glorify God (Romans 15:5-6)
- Keep our bodies pure and holy since we are temples of the Holy Spirit (1 Corinthians 6:19-20)
- Develop a mindset that our eating, drinking, and all things we do are for the glory of God (1 Corinthians 10:31)

The first four of the Ten Commandments (Exodus 20:1-11) are directly related to God's glory:

- **Have no other gods** - *"You shall have no other gods before me."*
- **Don't make or worship idols** - *"You shall not make for yourself an idol in the form of anything in heaven above or on the earth beneath or in the waters below. You shall not bow down to them or worship them; for I, the LORD your God, am a jealous God, punishing the children for the sin of the fathers to the third and fourth generation of those who hate me, but showing love to a thousand [generations] of those who love me and keep my commandments."*
- **Don't treat God's name lightly** – *"You shall not misuse the name of the LORD your God, for the LORD will not hold anyone guiltless who misuses his name."*
- **Keep the Sabbath holy to the Lord** – *"Remember the Sabbath day by keeping it holy. Six days you shall labor and do all your work, but the seventh day is a Sabbath to the LORD your God. On it you shall not do any work, neither you, nor your son or daughter, nor your*

2. Why Are We Here?

manservant or maidservant, nor your animals, nor the alien within your gates. For in six days the LORD made the heavens and the earth, the sea, and all that is in them, but he rested on the seventh day. Therefore the LORD blessed the Sabbath day and made it holy."

The real issue in glorifying God is recognizing that **life is all about Him, not about me**. When we truly realize this fact, giving glory to God is natural. I'll suggest three focuses we need to have in order to gain this perspective:

1. **Recognizing who God is** - The more we learn about who God is, the easier it is to give Him glory. In Isaiah 6, we see that Isaiah's response when he sees God on His throne is to glorify Him as the King, the Lord Almighty. This proper fear of God is needed because we sometimes become so "familiar" with the idea of God that we fail to glorify Him as He deserves. A lifetime of studying the attributes and characteristics of God will not only help us know Him better, but it will increase our ability to give Him glory for who He really is.

2. **Recognizing what God has done** - In Isaiah 43:7 God says He will gather His children *"everyone who is called by my name, whom I created for my glory, whom I formed and made."* As we discussed in the "R" portion of Origin, if God made us, He owns us. He not only made us, but he made the sun, moon, stars, earth, angels, gravity, souls, heaven, and even the ability to "think" about all these things. Reading history and biographies, taking a walk outdoors, looking through a scrapbook, keeping a journal of answered prayers, and many similar activities can help us meditate on the vastness of God's works. The more we recognize all that He has done, the more we can direct specific praise and glory to Him.

3. **Praising/Worshiping Him as He instructs** – Worship of God is a primary activity in Heaven and should be a primary activity during our lives on earth. We have a natural tendency to worship – people who don't worship God will worship something else instead. God's adopted children should worship Him properly.

   The study of worship deserves a whole book in itself. But here are a few thoughts:
   - I worship God with my entire life by offering myself to Him as a living sacrifice (Romans 12:1).
   - Worship is not as much something we do as it is who we are. God is to be worshipped in spirit and truth, and this is more a function of attitude and character than it is an event.
   - Praise is something that is visible or audible. The words translated "praise" or similar words in our Bibles describe actions or sounds that would be noticeable to someone around us.
     - For example, the second most common word translated "praise" in the Old Testament is "Yadah" (used over 90 times). Yadah means "to worship with extended hands, to throw out the hands" (Yad means "hand"). Our praise is not an internal-only thing – it should be noticeable to others.

O - Obedience to God (right actions)

Loving God is directly related to obedience to Him. Jesus said, "Whoever has my commands and obeys them, he is the one who loves me. He who loves me will be loved by my Father, and I too will love him, and show myself to him." (John 14:21) Since Jesus said it, I can be confident in stating the following:

To love God, we MUST obey Him.

Most Christians would agree with the statement above, but I don't believe most of us have REALLY pondered the significance of that statement. Let me make two other statements to illustrate this point:

If we don't make the time to study God's Word to see what He commands, we don't love Him.

If we know something that God commands and we don't do it, we don't love Him.

Those statements are not pleasant to write or read, but I believe they are as true as the first statement. God can choose to forgive us for laziness and disobedience, but as we willfully continue in these sins we are certainly NOT loving God. To love God in the way He tells us to love Him we must strive to grow in our knowledge of His commands and in our practice of obedience.

Here are a few practical suggestions on ways to better love God through obedience:

- Periodically select a book of the Bible and make a list of commands that apply to you. You might want to categorize them such as "commands I obey pretty well", "commands I disobey frequently", and "commands I didn't realize existed."

- Dedicate a time of prayer to ask God to reveal areas of disobedience in your life. Then ask for forgiveness, and ask for strength and wisdom in addressing those areas.
- Change your vocabulary about sin. I used to say "I struggle with that area" or "that's a weakness of mine." Now I try to say "I sin in that area, but I'm asking God to change me and trusting that He will."
- Honestly examine your heart and ask yourself why you DO obey God. Fear of punishment? Because you want others to think you are good? Ask God to increase your love for Him so that more of your motive is love and thankfulness.

D - Doctrines from God (right beliefs)

Right worship and right actions are dependent on right beliefs. The dictionary says doctrine is "a set of beliefs or principles held and taught by a Church, political party, or other group." To love God, we must hold to beliefs and principles that agree with what He has told us in His Word.

For example, what if we believe that people go to heaven because they do good things or because they go to church or because they are born into a Christian family? Our attitudes and actions related to the ministry of reconciliation (2 Cor. 5:18-19) will be affected by this belief. Our focus will be on getting people to "act good" or "go to church". If this is not what God says about salvation then we are not loving Him because we are living and teaching wrong beliefs.

Doctrines are often the basis for disagreements between Christians. We shouldn't want to have disagreements, and it is important for us to try to distinguish between the major issues and the minor issues. As much as possible we want to live in peace with others (Romans 12:18). But we must recognize that ***unity among believers is the result of pursuing truth, not the goal of our doctrines***. God's Word is our standard, and on a given topic there is a true doctrine/belief. You and I will have unity when we both find that truth. If we disagree, our pursuit of unity should be conducted with an open, humble, honest study of the relevant passages in the Bible (because we might *both* be wrong). We will not always arrive at the truth at the same time, but we should never forsake God's truth for the sake of "getting along." As one of my friends says, we should be able "to disagree without being disagreeable."

The topic of having correct doctrine is well beyond the scope of this overview. But here are a few suggestions on steps that can improve our ability to love God through our beliefs:

- Get a book that discusses the basics of the Christian faith. We've used R.C. Sproul's book <u>Essential Truths of the Christian Faith</u> and Bruce A. Wares <u>Big Truths for Young Hearts</u> as helpful read-aloud overviews of biblical doctrines.
- Get a systematic theology book for more in-depth study
- Review the creeds (such as the Apostles' Creed or Nicene Creed) that have historically been used in the church to summarize what are considered the basics of the faith
- Develop a concise outline of doctrine that summarizes those concepts that are major, worth dying for. Here's an example:
  - **God's Creation** - That the Triune God of the Bible chose to create time, matter, and energy and spoke it into existence. His original creation was perfect.

- o **Man's Sin Nature** - That God created man to have a special relationship with Him and promised man eternal fellowship if man obeyed God, but death if man disobeyed God. The first man rebelled against God's commands, and the result was that all mankind has been condemned to death and creation itself is in decay. God's standard is perfect righteousness, and no man meets that standard.
- o **God's Mercy in Christ** - That the divine Son of God, Jesus Christ, took on flesh, was born of a virgin, lived a life of sinless obedience, died a substitutionary atoning death, was raised again for the justification (restored relationship with God) of the saints, and is seated at the right hand of God making intercession for our sanctification (growth in holiness).
- o **Christ's Return and Restoration** - That Christ will someday return for all the saints. He will judge and condemn His enemies to Hell forever. He will perfect the saints (glorification) and restore His creation to perfection for eternity.

LOVING MAN

Loving people can be both easier and harder than loving God. It is easier because we can see people, touch people, share experiences with people. It is harder because all of us are very imperfect and our imperfections can be very aggravating at times. But Jesus said that the second greatest command is "Love your neighbor as yourself"." If life is about loving people, to fulfill our purpose we have to learn to love the people God calls us to love. We'll use the acrostic "MAN" to discuss key concepts in loving people.

M - Myself

"Love your neighbor <u>as you love yourself</u>." When you read that statement by Jesus you might have one of two reactions to the concept of loving yourself. You might think "Isn't that pretty natural?". Or you might think "Is this like that self-esteem psychology stuff?". I'm not certain how to interpret this "self" standard for the commandment, but since Jesus used this as the standard for measuring love for our neighbor we need to try to figure out what he meant by the concept of loving yourself.

My opinion based on other scripture is that Jesus meant that it is natural for us to focus our attention on our own interests, on getting what we think benefits us the most. When Jesus uses this as the standard for loving our neighbor he may be saying "you automatically look to your own interests, so look to the interests of your neighbor with the same passion." This is said another way in Philippians 2:4 "Each of you should look not only to your own interests, but also to the interests of others." Or again Jesus said "So in everything, do to others what you would have them do to you, for this sums up the Law and the Prophets." (Matt 7:12) This seems to involve figuratively putting ourselves into the position of others and loving them by doing what we would want done for ourselves in that situation.

I think love as it relates to myself also has another dimension to consider. Many times we are tempted to do things that will give us short-term pleasure but that we know are ultimately bad for us (not in our best interests). We can consider the principle of ownership and realize that loving myself ultimately involves me doing what my owner wants me to do *because that will give me the best ultimate reward.* "Do you not know that your body is a temple of the Holy Spirit, who is in you, whom you have received from God? You are not your own; you were bought at a price.

93

Therefore honor God with your body." (1 Cor. 6:19-20) God offers us rewards and blessings for our faithfulness (e.g. 1 Cor. 3:14-15), so it must not be wrong to want to be blessed and rewarded. Loving myself by honoring God's conditions for giving me blessings can be a great motivation for me to make good long-term decisions rather than poor short-sighted decisions.

A - Associates (those close to me throughout my life)

The associates in my life are those people with whom I have regular contact and interaction. These include my family, my friends, my co-workers, fellow church members, etc. Loving my associates involves obeying specific scriptures about each type of relationship. Much of the Scripture that talks about relating to people involves people who are our associates. Here are some highlights of how we love these people:

- **Your Spouse** - Husband, love your wife as Christ loves the Church and as you love your own body. Wife, submit to your husband as to the Lord, acknowledging that he is your head as Christ is the head of the church, and so submit to him in everything. (Ephesians 5:21-33)

- **Your Parents** - Obey your parents when you are living under their authority, because God gave you your parents and obeying them is required in order for you to obey God. Honor your father and mother your entire life because this is commanded and because God promises you it will go well with you and you will enjoy a long life on the earth. "Children, obey your parents in the Lord, for this is right. Honor your father and mother"--which is the first commandment with a promise-- "that it may go well with you and that you may enjoy long life on the earth." (Ephesians 6:1-3) This is the fifth of the Ten Commandments.

- **Your Children** - Raise your children to know and love God and His standards. Be the major influencer in their lives because that is God's plan. Keep their hearts turned toward you so that you can protect them from evil influences. Teach them to be prepared for the roles God gives them as men or as women. Love them unconditionally and encourage/praise them so that they can better grasp the type of love God has for them. Do not exasperate them.

- **Your Employees** - Give them the pay they deserve. Value them as people, not just as resources. Don't ask them to sacrifice their families for their careers. Take responsibility for looking to their welfare as you expect them to look out for yours.

- **Your Employer** - Obey your earthly masters with respect and fear, and with sincerity of heart, just as you would obey Christ. Obey them not only to win their favor when their eye is on you, but like slaves of Christ, doing the will of God from your heart. Serve wholeheartedly, as if you were serving the Lord, not men, because you know that the Lord will reward everyone for whatever good he does, whether he is slave or free. (Ephesians 6:5-8)

- **Your Pastor/Elder** - Give double honor to those who direct the affairs of the church, especially to those who preach/teach. Do not entertain an accusation against an elder unless it is brought by two or three witnesses. (1 Timothy 5:17-19) Be submissive to the elders because they have responsibility for shepherding. (1 Peter 5:1-5) Obey your leaders and submit to their authority. They keep watch over you as men who must give an account. Obey them so that their work will be a joy, not a burden, for that would be of no advantage to you. (Hebrews 13:17)

2. Why Are We Here?

- **Your Fellow Believers** - Be humble with one another.
  If you see a brother in sin, point it out to him gently and
  with a humble spirit. Encourage one another. Pray for
  one another. Help meet physical needs of your
  brothers. Meet regularly with one another to share
  worship and a sense of accountability to God. Be
  considerate of "weaker" brothers and don't argue about
  minor things. Love as Christ loved us (John 13:34-35).
- **Your Friends** - Encourage one another to walk with the
  Lord. Be willing to lay your life down for a friend.

N - Neighbors (those who come into my life through situations like the Good Samaritan)

My neighbors are those people God puts into my life
because of proximity or because of circumstances. When a
self-righteous Jewish expert on the law asked Jesus to
define who his neighbor was, Jesus answered him with the
parable of the Good Samaritan. At the end of the parable
Jesus asked the expert which man was a neighbor to the
man who was abused by robbers. The expert rightly
answered "The one who had mercy on him" and Jesus said
"Go and do likewise." When a person truly needs help and
we're in a position to help, loving our neighbor involves
showing mercy:

- **Geographic Neighbors** - The people who live close to
  us are one type of neighbor. To love them we need to
  look for needs in their lives that we can meet.
  Philippians 2:4 says "Each of you should look not only
  to your own interests, but also to the interests of
  others." This may involve helping with some project,
  loaning some tools, bringing food during sickness,
  watching out for their home when they are away, etc.
  But we must also be careful not to force ourselves too
  much into their lives and become a nuisance. "Seldom

set foot in your neighbor's house-- too much of you, and he will hate you." (Proverbs 25:17)

- **Divine Appointment Neighbors** - These are people with needs who briefly come into our lives through unplanned encounters. We should always be sensitive to times when the Holy Spirit impresses us with a sense that we should help someone that we don't know. This might be someone in the grocery checkout line, a man sitting next to us on an airplane, a waitress who seems to need an encouraging word and smile. All of us have those moments of decision, and we need to trust God to lead us in responding correctly. "Do not forget to entertain strangers, for by so doing some people have entertained angels without knowing it. Remember those in prison as if you were their fellow prisoners, and those who are mistreated as if you yourselves were suffering." (Hebrews 13:2-3)

- **Secret Neighbors** - God often gives us opportunities to help people in a fairly anonymous way. Showing love to this type of neighbor lets us truly practice unselfish love since we don't expect to receive anything from them in return. Examples might include money or gifts sent to people in other countries, donating blood, praying for people we know only by name, anonymous gifts, and visits to nursing homes. These secret neighbors provide us with opportunities to lay up treasures and receive recognition in heaven. They are also an opportunity to minister with Christ. When you give a gift that only you and God know about, you feel closer to Christ.

"Then the King will say to those on his right, 'Come, you who are blessed by my Father; take your inheritance, the kingdom prepared for you since the creation of the world. For I was hungry and you gave me something to eat, I was thirsty and you gave me something to drink, I was a

stranger and you invited me in, I needed clothes and you clothed me, I was sick and you looked after me, I was in prison and you came to visit me.' Then the righteous will answer him, 'Lord, when did we see you hungry and feed you, or thirsty and give you something to drink? When did we see you a stranger and invite you in, or needing clothes and clothe you? When did we see you sick or in prison and go to visit you?' The King will reply, 'I tell you the truth, whatever you did for one of the least of these brothers of mine, you did for me.' (Matthew 25:34-40)

The last six of the Ten Commandments (Exodus 20:12-17) deal with loving associates and neighbors:

- **Don't Dishonor Parents** – "Honor your father and mother."
- **Don't Murder** - "You shall not murder."
- **Don't Commit Adultery** - "You shall not commit adultery."
- **Don't Steal** - "You shall not steal."
- **Don't Lie** - "You shall not give false testimony against your neighbor."
- **Don't Covet** - "You shall not covet your neighbor's house. You shall not covet your neighbor's wife, or his manservant or maidservant, his ox or donkey, or anything that belongs to your neighbor."

Enemies?

Jesus also tells us to love our enemies and to pray for those who persecute us (Matthew 5:44). By this we will show that we are sons of the Father and will be following His example. This is a hard saying for us – it's hard enough to love our neighbors even when they aren't enemies.

But when we apply the command to "love others as we would want to be loved" to the topic of enemies, we can see why this is consistent with God's character. *He loved us while we were His enemies – He's not asking us to do anything He hasn't done Himself.*

I - INCREASE

God created the process of growth, and a major purpose of our lives is to grow in various ways. Some areas of growth are natural, such as physical growth. Mental growth also just happens as we spend time experiencing life. But to accomplish our real purpose in life we have to continually and ***purposefully*** grow in the areas God commands us to grow. We'll summarize key target areas of growth via the acrostic "GROW":

- **G**odliness
- **R**elationships
- **O**bedience
- **W**ork

G - GODLINESS

When a Christian identifies himself with Christ he starts down the road to Christ-likeness. Growing in godliness involves growth in character qualities that are consistent with the character of Christ. He is our example of the ways we as humans can develop the "image of God" in which we were created. In one sense we can never be like God because He has attributes that we will never have. But apparently in some ways we can become like God, and Christ's life on earth is our model. We are commanded to be holy as He is holy (1 Peter 1:15).

Overflow of the Heart

The Bible refers many times to the heart and to what fills it. To grow in godliness requires *that I speak to my own heart and tell it what it should desire*. God says that our hearts are inclined to evil (Gen 8:21), but He also says that we can store up good things in our hearts (Luke 6:45). So I believe the action item here is to focus my attention on storing up good things in my heart so that the overflow of my heart will honor God. Good things are put into my heart through thoughts (Philippians 4:8), words spoken (Psalm 19:14), and words heard (particularly God's Words). As my heart is filled with God's good law, my desires and actions will be more godly (Proverbs 40:8). I want my heart to love what God loves, hate what God hates, and desire what God desires.

One practical step to take daily is to ask God to continually fill me with His Spirit (Galatians 5) so that the fruit of the Spirit (love, joy, peace, patience, kindness, goodness, faithfulness, gentleness, and self-control) is what comes out of me. I can't successfully focus on NOT being evil, but I can ask God to fill me with what's good (His Spirit) so that what flows out of me is actually fruit from Him. This allows me to be God-honoring even if I don't "feel" like it.

Pride and Self Worth

A common enemy of godliness is Pride. Pride is what Satan appealed to when he tempted Eve and Adam ("you will become like God"), and I think pride and self-centeredness are at the heart of most sins. As a Christian it is vital that I view myself with the proper perspective – I am a Beggar Offered Worth (acrostic of BOW):

- **B**eggar - On the one hand I deserve nothing. I am so imperfect and am capable of such wickedness.
- **O**ffered – Yet God has given and offered me so much.
- **W**orth - So I have infinite worth because God says He values me and has adopted me as His child and made me a joint heir with Christ!

To grow in godliness I need to recognize that my worth comes from God, and that what is best for me is to BOW before Him and serve Him rather than serve my selfish desires and pride.

MADE IN GOD'S IMAGE?

What does it mean to be made in God's image? I don't know all the ways we are unique in God's creation, but here are a few characteristics of man (in the acrostic IMAGE) that seem to be special gifts from God to humans:

1. **I - Imagination and creativity** – we can dream beyond what we have experienced
2. **M – Moral judgments** – we have a sense of right and wrong
3. **A – Abstract thinking** – we can think about concepts
4. **G – God-awareness and consciousness of self**
5. **E – Eternal spirit and soul**

R - RELATIONSHIPS

We have already discussed relationships in some detail in the previous section on love. But it is very important to emphasize the need for growth in our relationships. Unless we press forward and look to grow in our ability to be a better husband/wife, parent, child, etc., then we are squandering a God-given opportunity. Time inevitably causes change, and if we're not consciously seeking to make our relationships more pleasing to God then they will likely be changing in bad ways.

Thankfulness is often a key to our relationships. When we're thankful for people we do everything in our power to show them our love. When we take someone for granted we may not invest in our relationship until something (sickness, injury, frustration) threatens to take that person away.

My daughter Rebekah shared a profound insight with me yesterday. She said *"what if tomorrow the only things we had were the things we thanked God for today?"* If we apply this thought to our relationships it can help us remember to grow them through careful tending rather than let them wither through neglect.

Posterity
***Posterity will serve him**; future generations will be told about the Lord.* Psalms 22:30

The concept of "posterity" is a key aspect of our relationships. The term "posterity" typically refers to a person's descendants such as children and grandchildren. It can also refer to all the people that we influence for eternity.

We <u>will</u> have a lasting impact on future generations (intentionally or not). A man with several children may have hundreds or even thousands of descendants in a few generations. The children of the people he impacts can number in the hundreds of thousands. And when you include the future spouses of all those descendants you start to get a sense of the tremendous opportunity we are given to influence for good or for bad.

*Who, then, is the man that fears the LORD? He will instruct him in the way chosen for him. He will spend his days in prosperity, and **his descendants will inherit the land**.* Psalms 25:12-13

*....what we have heard and known, what our fathers have told us. **We will not hide them from their children; we will tell the next generation** the praiseworthy deeds of the LORD, his power, and the wonders he has done.* Psalms 78:3-4

So when we think about growing, we need to remember that we are growing a posterity based on our actions today. We should be purposeful in striving to have a posterity that will be a blessing to future generations.

O - OBEDIENCE

By nature man is a sinner, which means it is natural for me to disobey God. Some people think that we are born "neutral" or good and that disobedience is learned from our environment. People that believe that idea aren't being honest about their own hearts <u>and</u> likely have never been parents. No one has to teach infants to rebel and disobey – it comes as a standard feature. Obedience is a learned trait, and it is never perfectly learned.

Obedience is also not something that maintains itself. We are either growing in our obedience or we are slipping toward disobedience. Slipping away from obedience is a natural thing, but not a good thing. As Christians God gives us the Holy Spirit so that we can resist temptation to sin, but even then we don't always ask for that strength because sin is so attractive to us.

At our house we used to have some stuff we called "slime". It is a type of putty with incredible elasticity. It can ooze and stretch and mold itself for lots of fun uses (like sticking it on the ceiling and seeing how long it takes to stretch itself all the way to the floor). But this slime is always being pulled by gravity somewhat like we are always being pulled by temptation to disobey God. If you set a blob of slime on a stair rail or chair or anything it will start to be pulled downward by gravity. If you leave it long enough it will gradually work itself down as far as it can go until something stops it. The only way to keep it from doing that it is to keep pushing it back up or to close it up in a box.

This is an imperfect analogy, but our tendency to sin is somewhat like gravity and our obedience is somewhat like slime. To pursue obedience we have to continually push ourselves up in the strength Christ gives us to overcome our natural sin nature. We MUST be growing in obedience.

So how do we grow in obedience? We already covered some suggestions in the "O" section of Loving God. Here are four additional suggestions:

1. **Make yourself accountable** to a person who will ask you about your sins and obedience on a regular basis (at least weekly). Just knowing that you're going to have this discussion can help you resist temptation.

2. **Learn to flee temptation**. Ask God to show you what situations, people, and activities in your life provide strong temptations for sinful thoughts or action. Sometimes we don't need to try to get stronger in resisting a particular temptation. We just need to stop, turn it off, throw it away, or otherwise flee it altogether. Bob Schulz in <u>Boyhood and Beyond</u> recommends that when we're tempted we should ask the question "God, what do you want me to be doing right now?" and then go and do that instead of trying to fight a likely losing battle with temptation.

3. **Use the Golden Rule** to evaluate your words, actions, and thoughts. Would I want someone else to say those things, do those things, or think those things about me?

4. **Deal with sin in your heart before it takes root and bears bad fruit**. Since sin starts with thoughts, would I be ashamed if people knew what I was thinking? If so, I should ask God to change my heart so that I don't have to pretend my heart is different than it is.

W - WORK

God created us to work, and work is good. Before Adam sinned God gave him the responsibility to care for the garden:

The LORD God took the man and put him in the Garden of Eden to work it and take care of it. Genesis 2:15

After Adam's sin God said that his work would be harder, but work is still a good thing. Our culture says that work is to be avoided when possible, and that leisure (unproductive time) is our goal. But God created us to work. Whether we get paid or not, we are to be doing the work God has given us.

- **We have been saved to do good works** that God has prepared in advance for us to do (Ephesians 2:10)
- **We are to work with all our heart at whatever we do** because it is the Lord we are working for, not men (Colossians 3:23)
- **We are to work in the specific roles God has given us**. God gives distinct roles to men and to women, and our work should focus on fulfilling those roles. Our family acrostics for these roles are LEADER and HELPER:
  - The LEADER work of a man includes:
    - **L**eading
    - **E**lding
    - **A**ttaching (being a husband)
    - **D**efending
    - **E**arning a living
    - **R**earing children
  - The HELPER work of a woman includes:
    - **H**elpmeet to her husband or father
    - **E**ducator at home
    - **L**asting (spiritual) beauty

2. Why Are We Here?

- Producing godly offspring
- Enterprising at home
- Realmkeeping for her household

These are discussed in more detail in other writings.

- **We will be judged based on our works.** Our relationship with God is not earned, but we will earn rewards based on our work. 1 Corinthians 3:11-15 talks about our work being tested by fire, and if we have built our work on the right foundation (Jesus Christ and His Word) then what we have built will survive the fire and we will receive a reward. I don't fully understand this promise, but it conveys the concept that our work is important and will be judged.
- **We bring glory to God by the fruit we bear.** John 15:8 tells us that bearing fruit brings glory to God and shows that we're Christ's disciples. We don't cause the fruit (only God makes it grow) but we are responsible for planting and tending just like Adam was. All the farming and gardening analogies in scripture show that we are to be faithful in our part and that God will bring the increase. One of my pastors called it the law of the sower:
  - You reap what you sow
  - You reap more than you sow
  - You reap later than you sow

Jesus said, *"My Father is always at his work to this very day, and I, too, am working."* (John 5:17). Doing the work He has given us is part of the reason we have life.

F - FAITHFULNESS

The Bible makes it clear that one of the major purposes of our life is to be faithful. Being faithful in life means that we recognize and embrace our role as stewards. Everything we have has been given to us by God. He is the true owner of everything that I call "mine" ("If He created us, He owns us…"). What I "have" in this world is not mine to do with as I please. I have been given time, talents, and treasure for a season, and during this season I am to use them to bear fruit that will last.

My responsibility is to use the things I have been given in the way and for the purposes that He intends.

The parables of Jesus illustrate this powerfully, especially the parable of the talents:

"Again, it will be like a man going on a journey, who called his servants and entrusted his property to them. To one he gave five talents of money, to another two talents, and to another one talent, each according to his ability. Then he went on his journey.

The man who had received the five talents went at once and put his money to work and gained five more. So also, the one with the two talents gained two more. But the man who had received the one talent went off, dug a hole in the ground and hid his master's money.

"After a long time the master of those servants returned and settled accounts with them. The man who had received the five talents brought the other five. 'Master,' he said, 'you entrusted me with five talents. See, I have gained five more.' "His master replied, 'Well done, good and faithful servant! You have been faithful with a few things; I will put you in charge of many things. Come and share your master's happiness!'

"The man with the two talents also came. 'Master,' he said, 'you entrusted me with two talents; see, I have gained two more.' "His master replied, 'Well done, good and faithful servant! You have been faithful with a few things; I will put you in charge of many things. Come and share your master's happiness!'

"Then the man who had received the one talent came. 'Master,' he said, 'I knew that you are a hard man, harvesting where you have not sown and gathering where you have not scattered seed. So I was afraid and went out and hid your talent in the ground. See, here is what belongs to you.'

"His master replied, 'You wicked, lazy servant! So you knew that I harvest where I have not sown and gather where I have not scattered seed? Well then, you should have put my money on deposit with the bankers, so that when I returned I would have received it back with interest. "'Take the talent from him and give it to the one who has the ten talents. For everyone who has will be given more, and he will have an abundance. Whoever does not have, even what he has will be taken from him. And throw that worthless servant outside, into the darkness, where there will be weeping and gnashing of teeth.' Matthew 25:14-30

Here are a few observations from this passage:

- The master did not give each servant the same amount to start with.
- The amounts the master gave were based on each servant's ability
- The talents still belonged to the master.
- Both of the faithful servants received the same praise even though they didn't have the same total gain.
- Their reward was to be put <u>in charge</u> of even more things, which indicates that the additional things still belonged to the master rather than the servant.
- The unfaithful servant used his fear of the master as an excuse for disobedience and laziness rather than as a motivation for obedience.
- The parable implies that the servant with one talent could have received the same reward as the one with ten talents if he had just been faithful with the little that was given him.

Here are four related principles we can derive from these observations (and other passages in Scripture):

1. God owns everything

2. God gives each of us a unique set of resources and circumstances

3. God judges us on our faithfulness with what we have, not in comparison to others

4. If we are faithful with small things, God will reward us and entrust us with even more

To be a good steward requires more wisdom than any of us has, but God promises to give us the wisdom we need if we confidently ask Him for it:

If any of you lacks wisdom, he should ask God, who gives generously to all without finding fault, and it will be given to him. But when he asks, he must believe and not doubt, because he who doubts is like a wave of the sea, blown and tossed by the wind. James 1:5-6

We'll now look briefly at how we can apply these principles to the Time, Talents, and Treasures that God has given us.

TIME

Each day is a gift. None of us knows how many more days and years we have in this life. But God knows. He says that our years are numbered, and each of us will live as long as He determines. That leads to a simple conclusion:

If I'm still alive, God still has something He plans to accomplish with my life.

So how can I be faithful with the time I have? Let's apply the four stewardship principles above:

1. **I need to recognize that all of "my" time actually belongs to God.** The perspective I have on making decisions about how to spend my days determines whether I'm a steward or a thief:
    a. Steward question - "What does God want me to do with this time He's given me?"
    b. Thief question - "What do I want to do with my time?"
2. **My circumstances and available time are different than other people.** I have more legitimate demands on my hours than some people, and less demands than other people. My standard is not based on how other people use their time. To be a faithful steward I need to continually ask God for direction and have confidence that He will give me wisdom to make my days fruitful. *Trust in the LORD with all your heart and lean not on your own understanding; in all your ways acknowledge him, and he will make your paths straight.* Proverbs 3:5-6
3. **God judges my use of time based on the circumstances He's given me and I need to trust Him with the results.** God has limited me to 24 hours per day, and if I can't get everything done that I think I should then I'm trying to do too much. Sometimes He signs me up for "appointments"

that aren't on <u>my</u> "to do" list and these keep me from doing something that I thought needed to be done. But I take comfort from the thought that Jesus knows what it's like to be limited to 24-hour days. When He walked the earth He went to sleep at night even though there were people sick and dying that He could have healed. He said that He trusted His Father – I should also trust Him with my days.

4. **I need to be faithful with my days if I expect my years to count for something.** It is tempting to dream about great things we'll do for the Lord "someday" when the opportunity arises. But typically the greatest things we do are not one-time events. The greatest things we do are the result of faithfully using each day wisely and investing small amounts of time in worthwhile activities over a long period of time. Whether you think of it as goal-setting, daily planning, daily discipline, or something else, we all need to be reminded of why what we're doing today is important in the long run.

The writing of this book is an example of the pitfall of taking my days for granted. I started on this book over 25 years ago. I would never have thought it would take this long to finish a simple worldview outline. But because I didn't work on it a little at a time during my days, the years flew by. I'm looking forward to being able to give this book to my children, but I'm sorry I didn't have it for them sooner.

As long as I'm alive I should be using my days to accomplish what God gives me to do. It's easier to do this if I recognize that the time is really His anyway and that He will direct and enable me to achieve His purpose for my life.

Teach us to number our days aright, that we may gain a heart of wisdom. Psalms 90:12

TALENT

Another type of resource that God gives me is my talent. This includes the skills, abilities, and aptitude that I have received as natural gifts or have acquired through learning. Of course they are ultimately all gifts since even my ability to learn is from God.

Being faithful with talents requires very careful discernment because ***the existence of a talent is not proof that I need to be using it.*** Obviously if I am very good at something immoral (such as getting people to believe something that I know is a lie) then I don't need to be using that skill. And sometimes a skill is useful in some settings but not allowed by God in other settings (such as a gifted lady Bible teacher who can teach other women but shouldn't teach men). But many other examples are not as clear:

- ❖ If I am a gifted athlete, should I focus my attention on sports?
- ❖ If I am an excellent student is it okay if I don't go to college?
- ❖ If I'm gifted at teaching God's Word do I need to plan on going into "full-time ministry"?

Let's see how our four principles apply to talent:

1. **All talent is a gift from God and belongs to Him**. As with time, it's easier to make the right decision if you ask the right question:
    a. Steward question - "What does God want me to do with this talent He's given me?"
    b. Thief question - "How do I want to use my talent?"
2. **My combination of talents are unique and for a purpose.** Once again I'm dependent on God to lead me in using my talent to accomplish the unique purpose He has for me. I can't depend on my reasoning or the advice of others to decide how to use talents. Others will advise me not to "throw away" talent, but only God knows why and when that talent will be used in my life. My talents are not a reliable indicator of my life path any more than my

feelings are. Both of these need to be subject to God. It is nice to be "good" at something, but it is better to be useful to God.

3. **God's evaluation of my use of talent is based on the circumstances He has put me in.** I have the ability to do more than I have the time to do. He may not give me the opportunity to use some of my gifts in the way I would like to use them to get the results I'd like to have. But I need to remember that He is responsible for the results – I'm responsible for faithful efforts to walk in the paths He has prepared for me.

4. **The use of my talents should result in lasting fruit.** God did not give me talent so that I could pursue selfish goals. So if the only reason I'm utilizing a talent is for self-recognition I'm probably abusing the gift. The opportunities God gives me to use my talents will likely be recognizable because they benefit others and bring glory to Him (Love God and Love Others).

Sometimes we'll get recognition in this life for our talents. But since our talents are gifts entrusted to us from God, the important thing is to be recognized by God as a faithful steward of our talents. He is the only One who knows why we have our talents, so we can be confident that He is the only one who can direct us to use them properly.

TREASURE

The third area of resource God gives us is our treasure or material wealth.

"Moreover, when God gives any man wealth and possessions, and enables him to enjoy them, to accept his lot and be happy in his work--this is a gift of God." (Eccl 5:19)

Wealth (in the form of money and material goods) is a significant part of God's plan. It is both a powerful tool and a critical test in our lives. The Bible says as much about money and wealth as almost any other topic. Approximately 15% of Jesus' words are related to money and possessions.

Our four stewardship concepts for treasure are thus:
1. God ultimately owns all the wealth in the entire world.
2. God determines how much wealth we each have.
3. God evaluates my stewardship of wealth based on how well I do with what He gave me, not on how well I do compared to others.
4. My stewardship of wealth is a crucial test of my heart. The love of money is a root of all kinds of evil.

How do we honor the Lord in the area of treasure?

Here are five principles related to wealth (helpful but not exhaustive) that can be remembered with the acrostic "COINS":

C ontentment
Be content with the wealth God has given you. *"Keep your lives free from the love of money and be content with what you have, because God has said, "Never will I leave you; never will I forsake you." (Heb 13:5)* (See also Philippians 4:10-13)

116

- Don't set your heart on money. Avoid love of money (I Timothy 6:10)
- Don't seek happiness through money (Proverbs 3:13-14)
- Don't be motivated by greed (Proverbs 28:6)
- Don't be impatient - haste in trying to gain wealth leads to poverty (Proverbs 21:5, Proverbs 13:11), and debt is allowed but never encouraged (Proverbs 22:7)

<u>O</u> wnership

Be a steward of God's wealth that He has entrusted to you - acknowledge that it all belongs to God.

- Return first fruits as a continual reminder (Proverbs 3:9-10)
- Don't put your trust in wealth (Luke 12:16-21, Proverbs 23:5, Proverbs 11:28, Proverbs 27:24)
- Don't be prideful because of wealth (Proverbs 22:2, Matthew 19:23-24, James 1:9-11)

<u>I</u> ndustry

Be diligent in productive work regardless of your wealth - freedom from work is not to be our goal.

- Being productive with your gifts is required (Luke 19:11-27)
- Laziness leads to poverty (Proverbs 10:4)

<u>N</u> eeds

Be full of faith that God will supply your needs - know the difference between needs and wants. *"Two things I ask of you, O LORD; do not refuse me before I die: Keep falsehood and lies far from me; give me neither poverty nor riches, but give me only my daily bread. Otherwise, I may have too much and disown you and say, 'Who is the LORD?' Or I may become poor and steal, and so dishonor the name of my God."* *(Proverbs 30:8-9)*

- Jesus promised to meet needs (Luke 12:22-34)
- Paul testified that needs are met (Philippians 4:19)

S haring

- Be generous - share what wealth you have with others as God directs.
- Help the poor (Proverbs 14:31, Proverbs 22:9)
    - This is also a way to store up treasure in heaven (Matthew 6:20, Luke 12:33, 18:22)
- Share with those in need (Proverbs 28:22, James 2:15)
    - Especially other believers (Galatians 6:10)
- Leave an inheritance (Proverbs 13:22)
- Give according to your ability (Luke 21:1-4)
- Give cheerfully (2 Corinthians 9:7)
- Remember worldly wealth's ultimate worthlessness (Proverbs 11:4, Luke 12:15-21)

Our treasure or material wealth is Christ's test of our stewardship and faith in Him. (Luke 16:9-13)

Summary
To be successful in life I need to seek to be a good steward of what I've been given. May all of us who have been saved by God live our lives in such a way that at the end we will hear something like:

' Well done, good and faithful servant! You have been faithful with a few things; I will put you in charge of many things. Come and share your master's happiness!' Matthew 25:21

E - ETERNITY

Time is a creation of God. I am not capable of fully grasping the concept of God being outside of time, but I know that He is. The Bible begins with the statement "In the beginning, God created the heavens and the earth" so we know that God invented our concept of the time/space/matter reality from nothing. "In the beginning" is when God created time, the "heavens" are space, and "the earth" is matter.

So to understand why we're here it makes sense that we would look at why God created time and what effect our lives have on eternity. The three perspectives on time that we commonly use are:

- **Past**
- **Present**
- **Future**

Eternity is made up of all of these, so we'll look at them for answers to the question of why we are here.

PAST

"In the beginning" is the start of what we call the past. But even before (!?) the beginning there was always God. This is impossible for my mind to fully comprehend, but I need to remember that God is outside of His creation and is not limited by time like I am.

I believe a major reason for studying the past is the concept of **remembering** so that we develop a spirit of **gratefulness**. We have received God's mercy and grace and have lives that are much blessed. Many times the Bible tells us that people did evil because they forgot what God had done for them. If we develop a grateful heart from studying the past we will more readily trust God with our present and future.

So what do we see in the past that helps answer the question of why God made everything?

Universal Level

Before creation God purposed to create the universe and everything in it. The Bible records the major events and many personal examples of God working out His purposes in history. When seen in light of Scripture, we learn **Who God Is** and **What God Has Done** and **What God Requires** of us.

Here are key universal events in the story so far:
- ❖ Creation
- ❖ The first sin, which introduced death into the world
- ❖ The flood where God destroyed the original world because of their wickedness
- ❖ God's use of the Jewish people to be the priests and means of blessing for people of all nations and generations, and as instructors of what sin is
- ❖ The miraculous birth of Jesus and His earthly ministry where he modeled and clarified what God expects of us
- ❖ Jesus' death and resurrection as the final sacrifice needed to satisfy the penalty of death for those He saves
- ❖ The development of the Church as the body of Christ with the anticipation of Christ's return as Judge and Lord

So a possible answer to why we're here seems to be that *God created so that He could write a story that would demonstrate His Glory and His Love and many other attributes of Himself.*

Personal Level

Before creation, God chose those people He would save
from their sins and adopt as His children. Those persons
who know Him and have been saved by Him are part of that
group called "the elect" in the Bible. So on a personal level
the most important event of the past is that God chose me
to be adopted as His child (justification) and to live with
Him forever. ***One simple answer to the question of
why I am here is "because God planned for my life
before He created anything."***

PRESENT

The only portion of eternity that I can impact is the present. So my
primary focus needs to be on NOW. Since my lifetime is such a
small portion of eternity I'm going to consider the lifetime of a man
as being "the present" for purposes of this overview.

From a biblical standpoint this life (the Present) seems to consist
of:
- A series of tests and challenges and blessings to test and
  develop our faith.
- The only opportunity to be reconciled with God for eternity
- An opportunity to show love to God and others.
- An opportunity to do good works in service to the Lord (but
  not as a means to salvation).

Universal Level

The Present is a culmination of God's story so far and a
launching point for the next chapter of the story. God calls
for His people to be faithful and to trust in Him for the
results. He doesn't ask us to "manipulate" results by any
means possible. The Body of Christ is responsible for doing
what He tells us to do in the way He tells us to do it. As we
press on in obedience we are then to be patient as we wait

for Him to bring results at the perfect time. I believe the concepts of being salt and light and being ambassadors for Christ are the proper perspective for us to have regarding our time here on earth. We're not here to serve ourselves – *we're here to play our part in God's story and plan.*

Personal Level

In the Love, Increase, and Faithfulness discussions we've already covered most of the key aspects of how to live well in the present. I believe much of what God requires of us is outlined in those sections. The present is the time when God works out sanctification (making us holy) in our lives.

I am to be faithful in what God has given me to do now. He controls the results.

AN AMBASSADOR FOR CHRIST

When I try to get a general picture of how God wants me to relate to the world, the role of an ambassador is a particularly helpful perspective for me. The apostle Paul said:

So from now on we regard no one from a worldly point of view. Though we once regarded Christ in this way, we do so no longer. Therefore, if anyone is in Christ, he is a new creation; the old has gone, the new has come!

All this is from God, who reconciled us to himself through Christ and gave us the ministry of reconciliation: that God was reconciling the world to himself in Christ, not counting men's sins against them. And he has committed to us the message of reconciliation.

We are therefore Christ's ambassadors, *as though God were making his appeal through us. We implore you on Christ's behalf: Be reconciled to God. God made him who had no sin to be sin for us, so that in him we might become the righteousness of God.* 2 Corinthians 5:16-21

Here are a few observations about this passage:
- As ambassadors we don't view the world as citizens of the world. We are representatives of Christ and citizens of His kingdom, and we should view the world as He does.
- We have been given the ministry of reconciliation, encouraging men to be reconciled with the God Who made them.
- As ambassadors we should not have a fear of man, but a love and fear of the One who sent us. We share God's gospel on Christ's behalf for the good of those who hear it.

So when I view myself as an ambassador it helps me to view my life as God sees it and to view the world as a foreign place in which I've been commissioned to represent my King. This helps me overcome my tendency to fear man and his opinion of me more than I value God's opinion.

SHARING THE GOSPEL

Some Christians believe that the main purpose of our lives is to share the gospel with others to save them from Hell. I do agree that we are to be witnesses/ambassadors for Christ and to share the gospel as He gives us opportunities. But I don't believe God is sitting on His throne wringing His hands in worry about whether my neighbor is going to go to Hell because I neglected to witness to him. This is God's story, and He will save each person He intends to save. I should share the gospel because I want to see God worshipped by all people, not because I'm responsible for the salvation of others. I'm not capable of thwarting God's purpose for His people whom He chose before the foundation of the world.

For my children and grandchildren who read this, I pray that every one of you will be saved and that we will be together with Jesus forever. My specific prayer is that God has chosen each of you as His child. Make your days count by doing the things that will matter for eternity. Be faithful to God, and He will reward you forever.

The acrostic GRACE provides a simple outline of the gospel:

- **G**od - In the beginning God purposed to create time, space, matter, and life for His own glory. He also uniquely created man in His own image and gave man special dominion over the rest of creation. God promised man a path of eternal fellowship with Himself if man would trust and obey God, but warned that man would die if he refused to trust God.

- **R**ebellion - Man rebelled against God's command and chose the path that brought sin, death, and curse into the world. Because of sin, man deserves Hell and God's wrath. Since Adam and Eve were our first parents and representatives we are all born with a nature to sin and on the path to Hell.

- **A**tonement – God satisfied both His justice and His mercy by sending His Son Jesus Christ, who was fully God and fully man. Jesus atoned for sin by living a perfect life, suffered God's wrath and death as a substitute for us, and conquered death and sin by His resurrection from the dead. He also provided the Way for us to be restored to fellowship with God.

- **C**onversion –If we choose to turn from our sins (repent) and trust in Christ alone as Savior and Lord (believe) we are forgiven our sins and restored to fellowship with God. God is due ALL the credit because unless He chooses to give us faith (being born again) we will never choose Him. God not only forgives us but considers us righteous like Christ (justification), adopts us as His children (adoption), and makes us joint heirs with Christ.

- **E**ternity – After this life God will give us glorified and perfected bodies and will make us suitable companions for Christ for eternity. Both heaven and hell will showcase God's glory forever.

So Whose Choice Is It?

This is a topic that can be divisive and I raise it with reluctance. But I want to share what I believe at this point in my life and why I believe it. *I believe the Bible teaches that those whom God has chosen will choose to be saved.* I think this position is called a belief in the historic doctrines of grace (God's sovereignty in salvation).

Men I respect believe differently on this, and I used to believe differently. I also know I am capable of being wrong. This is not something we have to understand in order to live our lives in obedience to God – if we are obedient our lives will look the same whether we believe in free will or election. I grieve that this topic has so often become a source of argument and division. **It is important that we be able to explain the reasons for our position, but belittling brothers in Christ who believe differently is arrogant and wrong.**

It seems that the main objection to this position is that it is not "fair" for God to choose only some. This feels valid, but actually whatever God does IS right so this is not a reasonable objection. Some very bright and godly people think that everyone has a self-willed choice. *But, what is it that is in us that makes one man accept and another reject the gospel? And where did it come from?* In my opinion **what the Bible teaches is that the only people who <u>will</u> choose Christ are those whom the Father has chosen to save**. For example:

- Numerous passages talk about the elect and God's choosing them before the foundation of the world (e.g. *"For he chose us in him before the creation of the world to be holy and blameless in his sight. In love he predestined us to be adopted as his sons through Jesus Christ, in accordance with his pleasure and will—"* Ephesians 1:4-5 (also Romans 9, 2 Thessalonians 2:13)
- The Bible says that we are dead in our sins, not just sick. Dead people don't make choices. (Ephesians 2:5, Colossians 2:13)
- Jesus describes the process as being "born again" (John 3:3). No conception/birth was ever at the discretion of the "birthee".
- Jesus said that no one comes to Him unless the Father sends him. *"This is why I told you that no one can come to me unless the Father has enabled him."* John 6:65 (also John 6:44)
- Everyone who believes is born of God - belief is a sign of being saved, not the means. *"Everyone who believes that Jesus is the Christ is born of God, and everyone who loves the father loves his child as well."* 1 John 5:1

There are many well-known verses related to salvation that talk about people calling on Christ and believing in Him and having faith, but I don't believe these necessarily teach that the calling, believing, or faith comes from an autonomous human will. The Bible teaches that **these are a gift from God** (e.g. Ephesians 2:8-9), and unless God gives the gift of faith, no one who is dead in his sins will ever choose to be saved.

So the bottom line is that I currently believe **we all do have a choice, but we won't choose to repent and receive salvation unless we've first been chosen and given faith and made alive by God**. God will not reject any who come to Him, but the only ones who seek Him have first been drawn <u>by</u> Him.

FUTURE

People have always been fascinated with the prospect of knowing the future. Compared to the past and the present, most of our existence will be spent in the future. Understanding life and why we're here depends on an understanding of the future.

Universal Level

Everything we've said to this point makes this fairly easy to summarize. God will continue to develop His story until He is ready for the closing act. In the Bible we get a revelation of what that act will be like, and it is gloriously awesome and terrible. Jesus Christ will return to earth to rule and to judge. God will gather His chosen people from all of history and will pour out his wrath on His enemies. God will finally satisfy His justice against evil, and it will be a terrible thing to watch and an unbearable thing to experience. God will then destroy the world in fire and recreate it for an eternal dwelling place for His people and Himself.

The timing and details of Christ's return and God's judgment and restoration are much debated. Many folks smarter than I am have studied this extensively and reached different conclusions, so I don't think God gave us enough info to be sure of the details. But we do know this:

The good guys win, the bad guys lose, and God's purpose will be accomplished exactly as He planned it before the time of creation.

Personal Level

My personal destiny is a subset of the Universal one. If I am one of God's adopted children then I will spend my eternal future in God's presence enjoying His blessings and doing His work. If I have not been reconciled to God then I will spend my eternal future in Hell suffering the just punishment for my sins.

Many people have decided to reject this idea because they don't think it is fair. As we saw in the introduction to this book, there is no logical way to arrive at a standard of "fairness" apart from God. What God does is right because God is entirely righteous. Whether we like God's plan is not the point. It is true, and it will happen.

The brief glimpse of heaven that we're given suggests that we will serve and enjoy God forever. We won't be bored or unhappy or suffering, but will live in the joy and beauty of Christ Himself. Because we will be glorified and given perfected bodies (glorification) we should expect the future of God's saints to be one of incredible **fruitfulness**.

Praise God for the hope He has given us for our future!

From eternity past to eternity future we are part of God's plan and part of the Story He has written. *Gratefulness for the past and Faithfulness for the present will lead to Fruitfulness in the future.*

ONLY TWO DESTINATIONS

The Bible teaches that every person will spend eternity in either Heaven or Hell. There are no other options. We don't just cease to exist as some people want to believe. We don't get reincarnated so we can try again to get it right. Those who have been born again through faith in Jesus Christ will be in Heaven, everyone else will be in Hell. That seems to be the clear teaching of Scripture. Jesus said that the path to life goes through a narrow and small gate and only a few will find it, while the road that leads to destruction is broad and the gate is wide and many will go that way. I understand this to mean that the majority of people from all time will be in Hell, and the minority will be in Heaven. Or at least that appears to be the implication.

Heaven is described as a place where there will be no more tears and sorrow, a place where we will live in the light of God's presence forever with the river of life and tree of life readily available to us. God didn't give us a lot of details, but since we will live with Christ it must be a pretty special place. It will be wonderful enough to keep us content and joyful for eternity.

Hell is the place where God punishes sinners forever. It is described as a place of torment and agony and unquenchable fire. I've heard people say that Hell is eternal separation from God, but I don't think that this means the *absence* of God. God is present everywhere, yet His presence in Hell will not be as the merciful and longsuffering provider of sun and rain and blessings that unbelievers have experienced in this life. God's presence in Hell will be as the righteous, holy, wrathful, and all-powerful Bringer of Justice upon sinners. When we see glimpses of the wrath of God in Revelation we see why an eternity of God's wrath is unimaginably horrible.

LIFE RECAP

To answer the question of why we are here, we use the acrostic LIFE:

Love

The greatest commandments are to love God and to love others.

- GOD - We love God through right perspective (His **G**lory), right actions (**O**bedience), and right thinking (**D**octrine).
- MAN – We love man through proper actions toward **M**yself, toward **A**ssociated people, and toward **N**eighbors

Increase

We are to purposefully seek **GROW**th in all areas of our life.

- **G**odliness
- **R**elationships
- **O**bedience
- **W**ork

Faithfulness

We are to be faithful with our Time, Talent, and Treasure since we are really just stewards of these things God has given us.

Eternity

God created time and is not limited by it.

- Past – Remembering leads to Gratefulness
- Present - In the Present we can pursue Faithfulness
- Future - In the Future we look for Fruitfulness

REVIEW

We are all biased - Our answers to life's big questions are based 99.99% on our bias, our assumptions about the "whole ball" that we don't know first-hand.

- If there is Someone who knows the whole ball it is logical to get our answers from Him.
- If there is no one who knows it all we have to rely on our reason, which would be the result of random, purposeless accidents.

Beginnings - ORIGIN

- **O**nly Two Choices
- **R**ealize the Significance
- **I**s it Faith or Science?
  - o LAB - **L**ookable, **A**ccessible, **B**reakable
- **G**uess at the Evidence
- **I**nspect the Evidence
  - o Universe = **"Decay"**
  - o Age of the Earth = **"Can't Say"**
  - o Origin of Life by Chance = **"No Way"**
  - o Evolution of Species and Man = **"Lacks Genes and Tweens"**
- **N**o Compromise - DON'T
  - o **D**eath after man, not before
  - o **O**rder of Creation
  - o **N**ames in genealogies define timeframe
  - o **T**en Commandments refer to seven-day week

Intent of Life – LIFE

- **L**ove - GOD and MAN
  - o **G**lory of God (right perspective)
  - o **O**bedience to God (right actions)

- o   **D**octrines of God (right thinking)
- **I**ncrease – GROW
  - o   **G**odliness
  - o   **R**elationships
  - o   **O**bedience
  - o   **W**ork
- **F**aithfulness - Time, Talent, Treasure
  - o   God owns everything
  - o   God gives each of us unique circumstances
  - o   God judges us on our faithfulness with what we have, not in comparison to others
  - o   If we are faithful with small things, God will reward us and entrust us with even more
- **E**ternity – Past, Present, Future
  - o   Past - Gratefulness
  - o   Present - Faithfulness
  - o   Future - Fruitfulness

.....still to come...
Authority
Standards

3. WHO'S IN CHARGE?
Authority - The Ultimate P.O.W.E.R.

This question deals with the nature of whatever power we think is in control of the universe. Some think there is no god, that chance and random forces determine what happens. Others think that Mother Nature (natural processes) is in charge. Others think that there is a god, but the god they imagine is very different from the God of the Bible. ***The God of the Bible is the True God.***

In this chapter I want to highlight a few of the attributes of the True God that help distinguish Him from other false gods and ideas. Like the rest of this book we'll just skim the surface of this topic, but I hope this will be helpful in contrasting the True God to the concept of god found in other religious beliefs and worldviews.

What we know about the True God is only what He has revealed to us. Since God is outside of creation we can't go to Him – He has to come to us. But He has revealed much about Himself. We'll look at a few names He gives to Himself and discuss some attributes He reveals to us.

But before we continue I want to point out four serious but unavoidable shortcomings of this approach to studying God:

God is a unified being and can't be "dissected" for easy study.

Despite all God has told us about Himself, we don't even begin to grasp Who He Is. When Moses asked how he should explain God to the Israelites, God said to just tell them "I AM" sent him. God is, and there is nothing to compare to Him.

God is not like us, and we tend to view Him as if He is

In Psalm 50:21 God rebukes the wicked by saying *"you thought I was altogether like you."* We need to remember that we tend to try to understand God by comparing Him to us. That's understandable, but inadequate.

God is perfect, and anything we don't "like" about Him simply reveals that we are NOT perfect.

All of His attributes are perfect and are perfectly in harmony. We can't pick and choose which ones we like. As overwhelming as the individual characteristics of God are, GOD is infinitely more. His justice and His mercy, His grace and His wrath, all of it is just right. He is worthy of all our worship and praise and adoration and admiration. My goal here is simply to be ready to explain some notable characteristics of God that provide glimpses of His perfection.

The ultimate purpose of our study is not to know about Him

The proper purpose of studying God is to know Him in an ever-deepening relationship.

God's Names

In the Bible God uses different names for Himself to reveal different aspects of His character. Our English-translation Bibles mask some of the variety in these names. Here are some of the more common names God has in the original texts that are typically translated "Lord" in our bibles:

Jehovah-tsidkenu	"The Lord My Righteousness" - God is the one who makes us righteous (2 Cor 5:21)
Jehovah-m'kaddesh	"The Lord Who Sanctifies" - God is the one who sets us apart for His purpose (Rom 8:28-30)
Jehovah-shalom	"The Lord is Peace" - God gives us peace (Is 26:3-4)
Jehovah-shammah	"The Lord is There" - God is always with us (Psalm 139:1-12)
Jehovah-rophe	"The Lord Who Heals" - God is our healer and the Great Physician (Psalm 147:3)
Jehovah-jireh	"The Lord's Provision Shall Be Seen" - God is the provider for all our needs (Philippians 4:19)
Jehovah-nissi	"The Lord My Banner" - God is the banner that goes before us and we follow his lead (Ex 17:15-16, Is 13:2-4,11)
Jehovah-rohi	"The Lord My Shepherd" - God is our shepherd who continually watches over us and guides us (Psalm 23)

These and other names give us insight into how God wants us to view Him and trust Him. We ask Him for help, and He gives us Himself as the Holy Spirit. *He offers in Himself the things that our hearts most desire to have* – righteousness, peace, comfort, healing, provision, leadership, a meaningful purpose, and Someone to take care of us.

The POWER acrostic below covers some key attributes of God that can be memorized for ready comparison to the gods of other worldviews:

- **P**ersonal and Loving
- **O**mnipotent
- **W**ise and All-Knowing
- **E**verywhere and Eternal
- **R**ighteous and Reliable

P - PERSONAL AND LOVING

So God created man in his own image, in the image of God he created him; male and female he created them. Genesis 1:27

This is love: not that we loved God, but that he loved us and sent his Son as an atoning sacrifice for our sins. 1 John 4:10

These are some of the most distinctive characteristics of God when compared to other gods.

PERSONAL
God is a person, actually Three Persons in One. While other worldviews talk about universal powers and impersonal gods ruling over them, God the Creator chooses to have personal relationships with His creatures. He calls certain people His "friends" and His "children". The personhood of God is an amazing and unique characteristic. God made man "in His own image" and the fact that we are persons with personality is simply the result of God transferring to us something that He has Himself.

LOVING
God is the source of all love, and the Bible even says that God <u>is</u> love (1 John 4:16). So not only does God have all authority over us, but He actually **loves** us even though He knows all the reasons that we don't deserve to be loved. This is most evidenced by His mercy to us in salvation.

*As for you, you were dead in your transgressions and sins, in which you used to live when you followed the ways of this world and of the ruler of the kingdom of the air, the spirit who is now at work in those who are disobedient. All of us also lived among them at one time, gratifying the cravings of our sinful nature and following its desires and thoughts. Like the rest, we were by nature objects of wrath. **But because of his great love for us, God**, who is rich in mercy, made us* *alive with Christ even when we were dead in transgressions--it is by grace you have been saved. And God raised us up with Christ and seated us with him in the heavenly realms in Christ Jesus,* Ephesians 2:1-6

What an amazing demonstration of love we see in this passage:

- The creatures God made rebelled against Him...

- ... and were dead in their sins deserving His wrath...

- ...yet He sent His son to die for those dead sinners...

- ...and raised them up to a favored place in His kingdom!

God makes it clear that the loving mercy He gives us in salvation is totally undeserved and is not based on works at all. He loves because it is His nature, not because we deserve it.

Related attributes of God include:

- **Patience** – His willingness to delay His judgment

- **Grace** – His giving to us good things that we don't deserve, particularly forgiveness of sins and adoption as His children

- **Mercy** – His compassion toward us by not giving us the consequences of sin that we rightfully deserve.

Within Appendix B there is a chart that contrasts a Christian worldview with some other major worldviews. The following excerpt illustrates the uniqueness of God's personal and loving nature:

	The Nature of God
Biblical Christianity	***Personal and loving Trinity***
Hinduism	Impersonal force
Buddhism	Impersonal force
Roman Catholicism	Personal and loving Trinity
Confucianism	Impersonal force
Judaism	Creator and Ruler of the World
Islam	Impersonal being
Atheism, Agnosticism, Skepticism	Deny existence or don't know
Marxism	Deny existence
Secular Humanism	Deny existence or unimportant
New Age Movement	God is all and we are all God
Mormonism	Evolved man – not a Trinity
Jehovah's Witnesses	Personal god – not a Trinity
Transcendental Meditation	Impersonal – all is God
Unification Church/"Moonies"	God is dual – male/female
Christian Science	God is creation itself

THE TRINITY - THREE IN ONE

The Personal nature of God includes the concept of the Trinity, a unique and wonderful and puzzling concept. I can't fully understand it and certainly can't explain it. Every analogy I've heard is flawed. But God tells us that He is One in Three Persons so I've outlined the key points with the acrostic "ONE":

O - Only One God

The Bible clearly teaches that there is only one God. *"You were shown these things so that you might know that the LORD is God; besides him there is no other."* (Deut 4:35, also Deut 6:4, Mark 12:29)

N - Numerous Nature of God in Three Persons

The Bible teaches that there are three distinct personalities within the nature of God. Scripture doesn't try to explain how God could have three persons and be one God – it just says that it is so. For example, we can see the three personalities at work:

In the resurrection of Christ
- God the Father raised Christ from the dead (Romans 6:4)
- Jesus was raised by his own power (John 10:17-18)
- Jesus was made alive by the Holy Spirit (Romans 8:11)
- The Three Persons work as One (Matthew 28:19)

In creation
- God created the universe (Genesis 1:1)
- God the Father created (Matthew 25:34)
- God the Son created (Colossians 1:15-16)
- God the Spirit created (Psalm 104:30)

E - Equality of Persons - They are all God
The Bible teaches that all three of the persons of God are equally God.
- God the Father is God (Gal 1:1)
- God the Son is God (John 1:1)
- God the Spirit is God (Acts 5:3-4)

O - OMNIPOTENT

Our God is in heaven; he does whatever pleases him. Psalm 115:3

Omnipotent means that ***God is All-Powerful – He has the ability to do anything He purposes to do.*** It seems very logical that the One Who simply spoke everything into existence and is outside of creation would have total authority and power over that creation. Yet even though it is logical, we can't really grasp the extent of "All Powerful" because we can't measure it or compare it to anything else.

Most people instinctively recognize that God must be all-powerful or He wouldn't be God. If He wanted to do something but couldn't, that would be pitiable. But as a practical matter we sometimes act as if God is limited in His power. If we say that we know God wants to fix a situation or wants to give us something but then He doesn't, we're implying that His power is insufficient. But His power IS sufficient. When we don't receive what we ask for it is solely because He purposed not to give it to us, not because He is unable.

The only "limits" to what God can do are the limits He places on Himself because of His character. For example:

- God cannot sin

- God cannot break His promise

- God will not forsake His people

- God will not ignore any aspect of his character (His compassion does not eliminate His justice, His justice does not eliminate His love)

Most other worldviews that include a god also believe that their god is omnipotent. But for the worldviews that deny a god, this is a key difference. A personal God with all power is THE authority because He has unlimited ability to do what He chooses.

GOD'S SOVEREIGNTY

*For **God is the King of all the earth**; sing to him a psalm of praise. God reigns over the nations; God is seated on his holy throne.*
Psalms 47:7-8

A related attribute of God is His sovereignty. This refers to His absolute rule over creation, including nations and individuals. He is the King of Kings and Lord of Lords – ***He has both the authority to decide all matters and the power to implement His decisions.*** This again is consistent with His character – He has universal authority over everything, everybody, everywhere, always.

Some people object to God's sovereignty because they believe it eliminates man's freedom. In one sense that is true. God's rule is absolute – man's will does not override God's sovereignty.

But I think this objection begs a follow up question – man's freedom to do *what*? If God is <u>not</u> sovereign, man is:

- "Free" to be randomly attacked, killed, plundered, and otherwise subjected to the "freedom" of other men and nations without God's control

- "Free" to suffer death, disease, calamity, and suffering knowing that it is totally random and purposeless

- "Free" to continue in rebellion against God and suffer eternal punishment in Hell because God doesn't "interfere" with souls that are dead in sin.

A sovereign God is in control – nothing happens to us without His permission. A non-sovereign god would be more like a super-hero – he could ride in to rescue us occasionally but he couldn't rescue everyone at the same time from all danger and calamity.

It's fairly easy to see God's sovereignty in creation (unless you believe in Mother Nature or random chance). No rational person believes that man has sovereign control over a tornado, the waves of the ocean, a lightning bolt, or the sun. These obey God alone. But we sometimes fail to realize that it's even more foolish to believe that a man could thwart the eternally-determined purpose of the Almighty. We need to rejoice in the fact that God is sovereign and that He will accomplish His purpose in our lives. ***Our lives are not only under His control, but they are also under His watchful care and loving direction.***

W - WISE AND ALL-KNOWING

Oh, the depth of the riches of the wisdom and knowledge of God! How unsearchable his judgments, and his paths beyond tracing out!
Romans 11:33

KNOWLEDGE

We started this book with the thought that God has all knowledge for all time (and even before time). There is nothing that God does not know. But that still understates His perfect knowledge (omniscience). Not only does God know everything, but He has never needed to learn, has never been surprised, and has never needed additional input. His knowledge has always been complete. ***There is nothing God does not know, and He has always known it.***

God's knowledge is perfect. Only an infinite Being could possess infinite knowledge, and as creatures we can only marvel at it. But God's omniscience has a very different consequence for believers than for unbelievers:

- **For believers** this means that God knows everything about us (our thoughts, our sins, our grief, our joy, our desires, our temptations), *yet He loves us anyway.* We don't have to worry about Him finding out something about us that He didn't know – He knows it all and still chose us as His children.

- **For unbelievers** this means there is no place to hide (Psalm 139:7, 11, 12) and no escaping the consequences for sin. What a terrible situation – a holy and righteous God knows the very motives of your heart as well as your actions. There will be no excuses that will avail and all who fall under God's wrath will know that it is just. This is probably one of the main reasons people want to reject the idea of God – an all-knowing God is frightening to His enemies. If this causes you to want to flee to God, praise God because only He can give you that desire. Throw yourself on His mercy and He will grant it to you.

WISDOM

God's wisdom is the perfect utilization of His knowledge. Our pastor recently defined God's wisdom as:

God always does the right thing, in the right way, for the right reasons, at precisely the right time.

When we think of wisdom we usually think of a person who makes good decisions and who gives useful advice. But God's wisdom is not just a larger version of man's wisdom. God is the standard for wisdom – something is wise because it is a reflection of God's counsel. We can't evaluate God's wisdom because there is no other standard to use for wisdom.

I believe we often don't recognize that God's Wisdom is just as amazing as His Knowledge. Because we recognize that God knows everything, it just seems natural that He would be wise. But if we think about it, we know that wisdom is something totally different. If we could build an infinite computer and input all possible data into it, would it be wise? Of course not. It would have access to information, but it would have no ability to use that information "wisely".

What a comfort it is (to those who are reconciled to Him) to know that the Power in charge of the world knows everything <u>and</u> is perfectly able to use that knowledge to accomplish His purposes.

Receiving God's Wisdom

All wisdom is found in God, but He offers to share it with us.

"The fear of the LORD is the beginning of wisdom, and knowledge of the Holy One is understanding." (Proverbs 9:10).

If any of you lacks wisdom, he should ask God, who gives generously to all without finding fault, and it will be given to him. James 1:5

To obtain wisdom ourselves we need to:

- Recognize that God is the ultimate Source for it

- Ask Him for wisdom

- Read His Word to learn what it means to be wise

E – EVERYWHERE AND ETERNAL

OMNIPRESENT

Can anyone hide in secret places so that I cannot see him?" declares the LORD. "Do not I fill heaven and earth?" declares the LORD. Jeremiah 23:24

When we consider that God is Omnipotent (all power) and Omniscient (all knowledge), it is inescapable that He is also Omnipresent (all places at the same time). He could not possess all power or all knowledge if He had to move Himself and His attention from place to place. ***God is completely everywhere at the same time.***

Let's consider how the fact that we are always in God's presence should impact us:

- **For believers,** when we are desperate for God's comfort we should recognize that He is there even if we don't "feel" Him. And when we are tempted to sin we should remember that He is right there as an ever-present eyewitness.

- **For unbelievers** this has the same terrible consequence as God's omniscience. God is right there witnessing every sin you've committed. He has seen all, and when you stand before His throne to be judged He Himself will be the eyewitness who testifies against you.

Remembering that God is omnipresent can be a great help in keeping us accountable for living our lives wisely. ***Wherever we are and whatever we're doing, God is always there.***

ETERNAL

"I am the Alpha and the Omega," says the Lord God, "who is, and who was, and who is to come, the Almighty." Revelation 1:8

We think of eternal as being a function of time – infinite past and infinite future. When we think of our destiny that makes sense.

But when we refer to God as being Eternal we mean even more. We previously noted that God is outside of time. So when the Bible calls him Eternal (such as Romans 16:26) I believe it is not defining him in terms of time, but in terms of His nature. To think rightly about God we have to recognize that when we think about God having an eternal past we tend to view it as an infinite past along a timeline. But God is not constrained by a timeline.

God described Himself to Moses as "I AM". God always has been and always will be.

Sometimes from our perspective it is useful to use terms such as "God was" or "God will be". But in God's Eternal Nature the truth is always "God Is".

Once again let's consider how this attribute of God affects us:

- **For believers,** we can rest in the confidence that God always will be. The promises He has made to His Church will be fulfilled because He will always be there to fulfill them. There will never be a "time" when God is not there. And in heaven we will enjoy His presence forever.

- **For unbelievers** it is terrible to know that the promised curses for the wicked will undoubtedly occur. God will not disappear from the scene. And even worse, He will pour out His wrath on sinners in Hell *without ceasing, forever.*

We are constrained by time in this life, and for our benefit God gives us a past, present, and future perspective. But when we consider the nature of God, the true perspective is…… **He Is**.

R - RIGHTEOUS AND RELIABLE

RIGHTEOUS

Your righteousness reaches to the skies, O God, you who have done great things. Who, O God, is like you? Psalms 71:19

God is righteous. To be more accurate, **God is the standard for righteousness because whatever He does is right.** This aspect of God is related to the fact that He is personal – we wouldn't even be considering His righteousness if he was just an impersonal force. But because He has personality and character we can say that He is righteous and holy.

We tend to think of righteousness in terms of what it is <u>not</u>. Righteousness is the absence of wickedness and sin and evil, and that is certainly true of God. But righteousness is not just the omission of sin. It is also doing what is right. The working out of His perfect power, wisdom, and love means that God is always doing what is righteous.

All of us consider ourselves to have varying degrees of righteousness when we compare ourselves to other people, but it is only in comparison to God's righteousness that we recognize how truly worthless our self-made "righteousness" is. Seeing God's perfect righteousness versus our sinfulness shows us that **what we deserve is death and Hell – anything we get beyond that is an unmerited blessing!**

Related attributes of God include:

- **Justice** – God is just, and His justice is perfect. He will not allow unrighteousness to go unpunished forever.
- **Holiness** – God is the standard for Holiness. *But just as he who called you is holy, so be holy in all you do; for it is written: "Be holy, because I am holy."* 1 Peter 1:15-16
    - o   He cannot abide with sinfulness. *You are not a God who takes pleasure in evil; with you the wicked cannot dwell.* Psalms 5:4
- **Wrath** – God detests unrighteousness and will pour out His wrath on it at the end of the age. The book of Revelation removes any doubt about this.

RELIABLE
Know therefore that the LORD your God is God; he is the faithful God, keeping his covenant of love to a thousand generations of those who love him and keep his commands. Deuteronomy 7:9

If we couldn't trust God as being reliable, none of what we know about Him would bring us comfort. Having an all-powerful, all-knowing, all-present being who couldn't be trusted would be terrifying. He would be like the mythical Greek gods who used their power for selfish and arbitrary purposes. Reliability is what lets us look to the future with confidence that what God said will come true.

God will always do what He promises. God does not forget, He will not change His mind, and nothing could possibly happen that will thwart His purposed will. By contrast, we often fail to do what we promised because we forget, we change our mind, or we are prevented by circumstances beyond our control. What a comfort it is to know that God is totally reliable.

Related attributes of God include:

- **Immutability** – God does not change, so we can rely on His promises. *I the LORD do not change.* Malachi 3:6a
- **Faithfulness** – We can place our faith in Him. *He is the Rock, his works are perfect, and all his ways are just. A faithful God who does no wrong, upright and just is he.* Deuteronomy 32:4
- **Trustworthy** – We can trust whatever He tells us to be true. *The works of his hands are faithful and just; all his precepts are trustworthy.* Psalms 111:7

But doesn't Scripture say that God changes His mind?

Certain passages in the Bible are said to indicate that God changes His mind about certain things or has regrets that He did something:

- ***The LORD was grieved*** *that he had made man on the earth, and his heart was filled with pain.* Genesis 6:6
- *When God saw what they did and how they turned from their evil ways, he had compassion and **did not bring upon them the destruction he had threatened**.* Jonah 3:10

These and other examples must be examined in light of other Scripture that talks about God's firm purposes (such as Isaiah 46:10). I believe we can see that passages like these are consistent with God's unchanging nature if we look at them more closely:

- In Genesis 6:6, God expresses sorrow over man's wickedness. Yet if He truly "regretted" creating man He would not have continued mankind by saving Noah and his family.
- In Jonah 3:10, Nineveh faced destruction because of their sins (like all men), but Nineveh repented and God showed mercy (like He does with us). We know from other Scripture that God was not surprised by their repentance because He causes repentance (e.g. 2 Timothy 2:25). So there was no "change" in God.

3. **Who's In Charge?**

WHERE IS GOD IN THE DARK TIMES?

Sometimes when we experience disaster and tragedy and despair in our lives it is hard to remember that God is Reliable. In our pain we want to demand an explanation from God just like Job did. It's not necessarily wrong to ask questions like "why?", but it is wrong to stand in judgment of what God allows in our lives.

My favorite analogy on this is that life is like a tapestry. God is weaving a beautiful picture from His perspective in heaven. But we see only the underside of the tapestry that is full of knots and loose threads and apparently random stitches. We can't understand what He is doing when we see it only from our side.

In his book <u>Trusting God</u>, Jerry Bridges offers a perspective that has been very helpful to me. He suggests that **in difficult times I focus on what I know for sure** (about God) instead of focusing on what I don't know (about the situation). What I know for sure is:

- **God knows everything**

- **God can do anything**

- **God loves me**

I can face my troubles with the thought "I don't know what good God is going to make from this, but I know that He knows about it, that He loves me, and that He is completely able to do whatever He knows is best."

POWER Recap

To summarize the answer to the question "who's in charge?" we use the acrostic POWER to outline a few of God's characteristics:

Personal and Loving

> God is three Persons in One and His very nature is Love.

Omnipotent

> God is all powerful – nothing is beyond His ability

Wise and All-Knowing

> God has always had complete knowledge, and He applies it in perfect wisdom

Everywhere and Eternal

> God is omnipresent and exists in all places at all times. He has always been and always will be.

Righteous and Reliable

> God is the standard for righteousness and holiness. He does not change and is always faithful to His promises.

Review

We are all biased - Our answers to life's big questions are based 99.99% on our bias, our assumptions about the "whole ball" that we don't know first-hand.
- If there is Someone who knows the whole ball it is logical to get our answers from Him.
- If there is no one who knows it all we have to rely on our reason, which would be the result of random, purposeless accidents.

Beginnings - ORIGIN
- **O**nly Two Choices
- **R**ealize the Significance
- **I**s it Faith or Science?
  - LAB - **L**ookable, **A**ccessible, **B**reakable
- **G**uess at the Evidence
- **I**nspect the Evidence
  - Universe = "**Decay**"
  - Age of the Earth = "**Can't Say**"
  - Origin of Life by Chance = "**No Way**"
  - Evolution of Species and Man = "**Lacks Genes and Tweens**"
- **N**o Compromise - DON'T
  - **D**eath after man, not before
  - **O**rder of Creation
  - **N**ames in genealogies define timeframe
  - **T**en Commandments refer to seven-day week

Intent of Life – LIFE
- **L**ove - GOD and MAN
  - **G**lory of God (right perspective)
  - **O**bedience to God (right actions)

- o **D**octrines of God (right thinking)
- **I**ncrease – GROW
  - o **G**odliness
  - o **R**elationships
  - o **O**bedience
  - o **W**ork
- **F**aithfulness - Time, Talent, Treasure
  - o God owns everything
  - o God gives each of us unique circumstances
  - o God judges us on our faithfulness with what we have, not in comparison to others
  - o If we are faithful with small things, God will reward us and entrust us with even more
- **E**ternity – Past, Present, Future
  - o Past - Gratefulness
  - o Present - Faithfulness
  - o Future - Fruitfulness

Authority – POWER – A God Who is:

- **P**ersonal and Loving
- **O**mnipotent
- **W**ise and All-Knowing
- **E**verywhere and Eternal
- **R**ighteous and Reliable

.....still to come...
Standards

Review

4. WHAT ARE THE RULES?
Standards - Knowing the R.U.L.E.S.
+————————————————————————————————

We all know that there are rules in life. From the time we're born
we are continually learning that one action is considered right,
another is considered wrong, if you do this then that will happen,
etc. The Rules we're talking about here are the foundational rules
of right and wrong. ***The Bible gives us these rules and states
that they are from God.***

In the time of the Protestant Reformation a major focus was on
"Sola Scriptura" – Scripture Alone. The Roman Catholic Church was
teaching that man's reasoning and traditions had as much authority
as the Bible. The reformers correctly argued that the Bible alone
was the standard for all truth and rules. If the Bible is God's Word,
it is not to be amended by men.

Our objective in this section is not to try to summarize all the rules
God gives in the Bible. The LIFE chapter summarizes some of them,
and Jesus summed them all up with the two greatest
commandments:

*Jesus replied: "'Love the Lord your God with all your heart and with
all your soul and with all your mind.' This is the first and greatest
commandment. And the second is like it: 'Love your neighbor as
yourself.' All the Law and the Prophets hang on these two
commandments."* Matthew 22:37-40

Instead of listing commandments we'll use the acrostic RULES to identify five general aspects of the rules found in the Bible. These five aspects can help us compare the standards of the Bible to other sets of rules promoted by other worldviews and people.

The Bible's rules are:

- **R**evealed (supernaturally) rather than derived from reason
- **U**niversal and apply to everyone, everywhere, all the time
- **L**oving
- **E**nforced
- **S**teadfast

As we discussed in ORIGIN, if God created us then He has the right to tell us what's right and what's wrong. Because our culture denies God's authority, it often denies His rules. As Christians we need to be ready to explain why God's rules are the standard to use.

R - REVEALED (SUPERNATURALLY)

All Scripture is God-breathed and is useful for teaching, rebuking, correcting and training in righteousness, so that the man of God may be thoroughly equipped for every good work. 2 Timothy 3:16-17

The Bible claims to be truth that God has revealed to us supernaturally through the Spirit-inspired writings of men over many centuries.

The reason we look to the Bible for answers to our four big questions is because we believe it is God's Word. As we discussed at the beginning of this book, God is the only One who could know it all. So we take His Word as the source of truth. To find out the rules for life we go to the revealed answers from God found in the Bible.

This is a stark contrast to most other worldviews. We live in a humanistic culture that believes that man determines the rules to live by, and that these rules are derived from our intellect and reason based on experience. In a post-modernist world we even deny that there are "real" rules and therefore we give ourselves a false sense of freedom to do whatever we'd like to do. Referring back to our "whole ball" analogy, this is the laughable effort of someone who knows less than a speck of the ball pretending he knows enough to override the authority of the One who created the ball!

Other religions have sacred writings that they also claim are supernatural in origin. Revealed truth is not a unique claim of the Bible. But because the Bible and these other writings are not in agreement on most topics, it is illogical to say that they can all be "true." Truth is absolute, not relative. The Book of Mormon says things about God and Jesus that contradict the Bible. Either the Book of Mormon is true, or the Bible is true. If the Bible is true, those other sacred writings are <u>not</u> true *at the points in which they disagree with the Bible.* Other writings may have truth in them (the Qur'an agrees that God created), but the standard of truth for a Christian is always the Bible. *For the word of the LORD is right and true; he is faithful in all he does.* (Psalms 33:4)

HOW DO WE KNOW THE BIBLE IS GOD'S WORD?

Why do we believe the Bible is God's Word? This is another topic that deserves its own book, but I'll try to give a brief but sufficient answer for our purposes.

This topic is similar to our ORIGIN topic because it is not absolutely "provable" in a scientific sense. So we'll use the "expectational" approach we used earlier. We'll look at what evidence we would expect to see if the Bible was true, then we'll inspect some evidence.

What would we expect to see?

Assuming there is a God who created us and who wants to communicate with us, what characteristics would we look for in a book/writing that is from Him? The Bible claims to be from God (2 Timothy 3:16, 2 Peter 1:21). But how can we know if that claim is true? Since the goal of this book is to provide easily-memorized points we'll simplify this to a familiar phrase. *We would expect God's book to contain "the Truth, the Whole Truth, and Nothing But the Truth".*

1. **The Truth**
    We would expect that everything written in the book would be true. This would include the areas of:
    a. History
    b. Science
    c. Prophecy
2. **The Whole Truth**
    We would expect that the book would sufficiently answer all of life's important questions.

     a.   It would answer the questions of where we come from, why we're here, who's in charge, what are the rules

     b.   It would be consistent with our observations of the world (including science and the nature of people)

     c.   It would provide a foundation for things we depend on such as laws of logic, uniformity of nature, and morality

     d.   We would not need any other "sacred" writings to answer these questions

3.   **And Nothing But the Truth** (so help us God ☺)
We would expect that the book would contain only the writings that God had inspired.

     a.   The "canon" or included writings would be accurate

     b.   The writings would be preserved accurately throughout time

     c.   The writings would be widely available and widely known

     d.   The writings would be consistent and would not contain contradictory statements

So, what do we actually see?

The Bible is the ONLY book that meets all of these expectations. The chart on the next page compares the Bible to other well-known sacred writings. Following the chart are some notes that provide more information on key points. For more details you can refer to books such as <u>Handbook of Today's Religions</u> by Josh McDowell & Don Stewart or <u>So What's the Difference?</u> by Fritz Ridenour. The following online links are also helpful:

- http://www.answersingenesis.org/articles/am/v2/n4/other-religious-writings
- http://www.comereason.org/cmp_rlgn/cmp005.asp
- http://www.equip.org/articles/bible-reliability
- http://debate.org.uk/topics/history/home.htm

Why Only the Bible is God's Word					
	The Bible	The Koran (Qur'an)	Book of Mormon	Hindu Scripture	Buddhist Writings
Claims to be from God	Yes	Yes	Yes	No	No
The Truth					
Supported by History?	Yes	No [1]	No [4]	n/a	n/a
Supported by Science?	Yes	No [2]	No [4]	n/a	n/a
Accurate Prophecy?	Yes	No [3]	No [4]	n/a	n/a
The Whole Truth					
Answers BIAS questions?	Yes	Yes	Yes	Somewhat	Partially
Agrees with observations of world?	Yes	Yes	Somewhat	No	No
Foundation for logic, nature, morality?	Yes	Yes	Yes	No	No
Only "sacred" writing with authority?	Yes	No (O.T. and Gospels)	No	Yes	Yes
Nothing But the Truth					
"Canon" is trustworthy?	Yes	No [1]	No [4]	Not known	Not known
Writings are preserved accurately?	Yes	No [1]	No [4]	No	No
Writings are widely available?	Yes	Yes	Somewhat	No	Somewhat
Writings are internally consistent?	Yes	No [1]	No [4]	No	No
(1) http://www.debate.org.uk/topics/history/quran.htm (2) http://www.answering-islam.org/Campbell/contents.html (3) http://answering-islam.org/Shamoun/false_prophecies.htm (4) See the two-volume work <u>A Mormon's Unexpected Journey</u> by Carma Naylor					

Related Notes:

The Bible

The Bible is a unified, consistent set of writings even though it is comprised of 66 books, written by over 40 authors, written on three different continents in three languages over a span of 1500 years. It is historically reliable, all prophecies that can be tested have proven accurate, and it is both internally consistent and consistent with reliable external evidence.

- As one example of prophecy, there are over 300 predictive references to the Messiah in the Old Testament that were all fulfilled in Jesus Christ. It is statistically impossible for this to happen by chance. The odds of just 8 of these being true in one person is 1 in 100 quadrillion (10^{17}). (Josh McDowell, Evidence That Demands a Verdict, pp. 166-167)
- William F. Albright, recognized as one of the greatest archaeologists, testified that there is no doubt that archaeology "has confirmed the substantial historicity of Old Testament tradition." (McDowell, Evidence That Demands a Verdict, pg. 65)
- The existing manuscripts for the New Testament provide overwhelming evidence for the accuracy of the text. The Old Testament texts were copied with painstaking procedures that make them also very reliable. (See McDowell's "Evidence" book for extensive documentation)
- I like the way the unity of the Bible is summarized in Answers to Tough Questions by McDowell & Stewart:
    - The Old Testament is the preparation (Isaiah 40:3)
    - The Gospels are the manifestation (John 1:29)
    - The Book of Acts is the propagation (Acts 1:8)
    - The Epistles are the explanation (Colossians 1:27)
    - The Book of Revelation is the consummation (Rev 1:7)

I also like the following description I heard in a talk by Dr. Voddie Baucham because it emphasizes that the Bible was written by eyewitnesses during the time of other eyewitnesses (who could have challenged the writings if they were false):

"The Bible is a reliable collection of historical documents written by eyewitnesses during the lifetime of other eyewitnesses. They report supernatural events that took place in fulfillment of specific prophecies and they claim that their writings are Divine, rather than human, in origin."

The Islamic Koran (Qur'an)
The source of the Qur'an is one man, Muhammad, who supposedly received it from the angel Gabriel. Early in his life Muhammad was likely exposed to different sects (and heretics) of Christianity as well as Jewish Scripture, and he apparently respected the Bible. At age 40 he started receiving "revelations" that were supposedly from God. It is very suggestive that at first he was convinced he was possessed by a "jinn" (demon). Muhammad was illiterate and did not write the visions down but transmitted them orally. A portion was dictated during his life and a portion was written after his death by his disciples. Only later in his life did he state that his teachings were from God and were replacing the "corrupted" version of the Bible, although the writings contain some inconsistencies and contradictions you wouldn't expect from God. Muhammad himself was a false prophet (research Muhammad's Satanic Verses for one example) so he is not trustworthy as a reliable source of God's Word.

The Book of Mormon (and other uniquely Mormon books)
The source of Mormonism's unique claims is primarily one man, Joseph Smith. Smith proved to be a false prophet on several occasions (such as his prophecy that the temple would be built in Missouri during his lifetime), which disqualifies him as a credible source for God's Word. Smith supposedly translated the Book of Mormon from some ancient writings he dug up with the help of an angel named Moroni. Some hieroglyphics he "translated" were later found to be nothing but Egyptian burial documents. In addition to the problems with Smith, the church teaches that the current heads of the church can receive new revelations from God, which means that no doctrines are completely settled or trustworthy. See the two-volume work <u>A Mormon's Unexpected Journey</u> by Carma Naylor for extensive documentation of the many problems with Mormon writings.

Jehovah's Witness Bible
I did not include this in the chart, but it's worth mentioning that the Jehovah's Witnesses have their own translation of the Bible that

has been modified to suit their doctrines. Examples include the denial of the Trinity, the related denial that Jesus is God, and the denial of Jesus' bodily resurrection. In addition, many of their founders who initiated these unique doctrines (such as Charles Taze Russell and Joseph F. Rutherford) proved to be false prophets as they inaccurately predicted the date of Christ's return.

Hindu Scriptures and Buddhist Writings
Since these do not claim to be from God (and don't even agree on a concept of God) these are not candidates to be God's Word.

SO...WHO WOULD YOU BELIEVE?

Any book is only as trustworthy as the author and his motives. Who seems to be a more reliable human author for God's Word?

1. A former treasure hunter who repeatedly made false predictions and whose mysterious translation of some hidden golden tablets gave him the benefits of a powerful position as head of a new religion? (Joseph Smith)
2. A man who thought he was possessed by demons when he received his first "revelations", had some "revelations" that were later retracted because they were thought to be from the devil, yet went on to proclaim himself as THE prophet who succeeded all other prophets? His ongoing "revelations" gave him enormous power as head of an empire. (Muhammad)
3. A group of men who gained nothing personally from their writings and who were often persecuted and killed for the ideas they proclaimed? (The men who wrote the Bible)

Life's true rules are revealed by God in the Bible, which contains *the Truth* (is all true), *the Whole Truth* (answers all of life's important questions), *and Nothing But the Truth* (is not mixed with errors and does not contradict itself).

THE CANON OF SCRIPTURE

One common question about the Bible is "how do we know the Bible includes the right books?" I'm not an expert on this, but I'll outline what I understand at this time.

The Hebrew (Old) Testament books were widely agreed upon in Israel. The Law, Prophets, and Writings (Psalms) Jesus referred to in Luke 24:44 included the books we now call the Old Testament. The Jews organized them differently than the Bible, but the text is the same. Christians simply adopted the writings that Jews accepted as being from God.

The Apocryphal books are NOT part of the Bible and were generally rejected by both the Jews and the early church. They were written 200 years after Malachi, they do not claim to be from God or to contain prophecies, and they contain doctrinal errors, sub-biblical morality, and historical inaccuracies.

The Roman Catholic Church leaders first accepted the Apocrypha at the Council of Trent (1545) primarily as a response to the Reformation and to use them as justification for some of their non-biblical doctrines.

The New Testament books were letters circulated among the early church, and the 27 books of the Canon were confirmed by the church at councils in the 4th century. These councils did not "decide" which books to include, but instead merely agreed upon which ones had already been validated by the church as being God's Word. Below is an acrostic CANON to summarize some "tests" they applied to verify that a book was from God. The book had to be:
- **C** - Consistent with orthodox beliefs and other scripture
- **A** - Apostolic in origin and Authoritative in tone
- **N** – Normally used (widely accepted by the church)
- **O** – Old and Original (in use since the early church)
- **N** – Inspired in nature (had the "feel" of authentic inspired writings)

U - UNIVERSAL

Those who devise wicked schemes are near, but they are far from your law. Yet you are near, O LORD, and all your commands are true. Long ago I learned from your statutes that you established them to last forever. Psalms 119:150-152

By myself I have sworn, my mouth has uttered in all integrity a word that will not be revoked: Before me every knee will bow; by me every tongue will swear. Isaiah 45:23

God's rules apply to all people in all places at all times.

The term "Universal" here means that the rules of right and wrong are absolute, not relative. God's rules apply to the cannibal in the jungles, the Buddhist of India, the Muslim of Saudi Arabia, the atheist of Russia, and the Eskimo in Alaska just like they apply to me. They apply now and they applied 4000 years ago and they will apply in the future. God's rules are not local or limited in scope.

Throughout the Bible we see that God has always judged nations and people as being "wicked" ***even though those nations weren't His chosen people***. Israel's enemies were punished for wickedness, yet they had not "chosen" to recognize or accept God's rules. This demonstrates that all nations and people are judged by God's standards whether they profess to believe in God or not. There is no option to choose another standard – God's rules always apply.

In recent years our culture in the United States has gradually adopted a value system that says everyone's beliefs are equally valid *unless those beliefs are considered intolerant.* This has resulted in a reluctance to criticize anyone's beliefs, no matter how crazy, unless those beliefs make an exclusive claim to being true (like the Bible does). At the root of this value system is the concept that rules are not universal, and that what's right for one person is independent of what's right for another.

In answering the question "what are the rules" it is <u>not</u> acceptable for a Christian to imply something like "I believe in the Bible, but it's okay for you to use a different standard." While it's true that God allows people to deny Him, His truth is still the only truth. As we've discussed, truth only makes sense if it is an absolute because:

- Logically two contradictory ideas can't both be true at the same time

- The laws of logic themselves are dependent on an unchangeable God who can give us a rational mind

The Bible is the standard for truth and the standard for right and wrong. Other worldviews may contain truth in the areas in which they agree with the Bible. ***But where other worldviews differ from the Bible they are wrong, and they are wrong for everyone, everywhere, every time.***

GOD'S RULES AND THE CHURCH

One application of this principle is that God's instructions to His people are not limited by culture, time period, or current trends. The temptation is to judge God's rules based on "current wisdom," an evolutionary bias that assumes we know more today than people did in the past. During the Reformation period in church history the Church made good progress in returning to "Scripture Alone" as the standard. But the Reformation left much undone, and the church today has adopted many practices and concepts that are not found in Scripture. Examples to evaluate include:

- Large church buildings funded by debt
- Youth groups and other age-segregated ministries that supplant parents as the spiritual authority and teachers for children
- Top-down leadership structures modeled after corporate organizations
- Program-centric ministries that try to meet all needs of all people via methods not supported by Scripture
- Women in the role of teaching and leading men
- Some "seeker-sensitive" churches that try to look like the world to attract worldly people in order to make them non-worldly (!?)
- Churches that are fixated on quantity of attendees rather than on depth of discipleship

Once again we see the temptation to make our reason our highest authority. If we are using models of ministry that aren't consistent with Scripture, we need to repent and revise. I respect what Paul Washer said when one pastor told him that his church would kill him if he tried to reform some of these cherished areas. He told the man, "then die."

L - LOVING

If your law had not been my delight, I would have perished in my affliction. I will never forget your precepts, for by them you have preserved my life. Psalms 119:92-93

God gave us rules that are for our good and in our own best interests.

Just as God is loving, so are His rules motivated by love. His rules are not capricious, selfish, ego-feeding, or designed to show off His power and authority. Again, this is an extension of God's character – God is love, so His rules are consistent with Who He Is.

This is an astonishing contrast with the other rule systems we find in the world. In most cases, governments and rulers advance their own interests ahead of the interests of those they govern. If a law increases the power and rewards for a ruler, that law is likely to be promoted by the ruler regardless of whether it benefits the people being ruled. This is really just a reflection of man's sin nature – by nature my first priority is pleasing me.

Our self-willed nature (the Bible sometimes uses the term "flesh) doesn't easily recognize the benefits of God's rules. When we want to do something and realize it is against God's rules we're like a small child - we don't like to be told what to do. But just like the small child we are fools in need of a loving parent to keep us from doing harm to ourselves and to others. That's the purpose of God's rules.

Let's look at the Ten Commandments as examples of some ways that God's rules are loving:

1. **Have no other gods**
   When we recognize that He is the only True God, we won't suffer all the consequences of a rebellious fool who puts trust in a false god.

2. **Don't make or worship idols**
   God designed us to worship Him. If we make an image of Him it will be less than Him. We will end up wasting our lives worshipping something vain and worthless rather than growing in our knowledge of Who He Really Is.

3. **Don't treat God's name lightly**
   Careless disrespect to God with our words promotes careless disrespect to God with the rest of our lives. The fear of the Lord is the beginning of wisdom. We benefit from wisdom and suffer from foolishness. God says that He is jealous for His name, and treating His name with honor helps us avoid suffering.

4. **Keep the Sabbath holy to the Lord**
   The Sabbath was instituted for us as a pattern of rest from work - the only reason God "rested" on the seventh day was to model this pattern. It was established for our good. Jesus said that the Sabbath was made for man, not man for the Sabbath, and that it is always proper to do good to others on the Sabbath. The Sabbath is an opportunity to pause from our work and rejoice in God's goodness to us, and to refresh our relationship with Him and other believers.

   Some Christians believe this command was not confirmed in the New Testament, so it is no longer valid. Even if that were true we still need rest. The Sabbath rest is a gift from God that reassures us that we don't need to work all the time in order to please Him.

5. **Don't Dishonor Parents**
   God promises blessings to us if we honor our parents. And

when we become parents we experience blessings again as our children honor us.

6. **Don't Murder**

   Life belongs to God. If others could take my life or the life of my loved ones whenever they wanted, it would be difficult to lead a peaceful and quiet life.

7. **Don't Commit Adultery**

   This rule protects the sanctity of a man and woman becoming one in marriage, and avoids the pain of a broken relationship and all the hurt this causes to other people (including children).

8. **Don't Steal**

   We enjoy the use of property that we own. It would not be enjoyable to live in constant fear of theft (just ask the people who live in cities where this IS a daily occurrence).

9. **Don't Lie**

   A world that is full of deceit and dishonesty makes life much harder because we are forced to constantly protect ourselves from the consequences of lies. If we can trust people to speak truth and to keep their word then we can be happier and more open with others.

10. **Don't Covet**

    One key to a happy life is to be content and thankful for what we have. It's okay to have goals that we're working toward, but if discontentment is our only motivator we usually won't be happy no matter what we get. To covet is to want something else so badly that we aren't thankful for what we already have. God tells us not to covet so that we can experience joy every day with whatever we have.

All of God's rules are in our best interests because God loves us and knows what is best for us.

E - ENFORCED

+_____

For if God did not spare angels when they sinned, but sent them to hell, putting them into gloomy dungeons to be held for judgment; if he did not spare the ancient world when he brought the flood on its ungodly people, but protected Noah, a preacher of righteousness, and seven others; if he condemned the cities of Sodom and Gomorrah by burning them to ashes, and made them an example of what is going to happen to the ungodly; and if he rescued Lot, a righteous man, who was distressed by the filthy lives of lawless men (for that righteous man, living among them day after day, was tormented in his righteous soul by the lawless deeds he saw and heard)-- **if this is so, then the Lord knows how to rescue godly men from trials and to hold the unrighteous for the day of judgment, while continuing their punishment.** 2 Peter 2:4-9*

God is just, and His justice requires that He punish sin.
Many people don't seem to believe this. There seems to be a popular and incorrect notion (even within the Church) that God is a tolerant grandfatherly being who, at the end, will bend the rules for us so that most of us can get into heaven.

The Bible tells us that God will not bend the rules and that no one will think him "grandfatherly" when He unleashes His wrath on sinners. God's justice is patient, but it will be satisfied. If God was going to bend the rules for us then there was no reason for Jesus to come to earth as a man and suffer and die for us. If God was going to ignore His own rules then Jesus didn't need to die. So the gospel itself is a stark reminder that God's justice is an unavoidable terror for those who continue in rebellion against Him.

The book of Revelation is full of images and descriptions that are frightening and gruesome. Even if we don't understand or agree exactly how to interpret Revelation, we should be able to agree that

God's wrath and power will be poured out on sin in ways that are difficult to even imagine. The scenes of Revelation show God bringing a series of punishments on those who rebel against him, each successive judgment worse than the one before. The rebellious will continue in their struggle against God until the end, and God seems to draw out the struggle to demonstrate His wrath. At the end Jesus simply speaks, and His words destroy the armies of His enemies.

For Christians the punishment for sin was paid in full by Jesus Christ. Our sins were attributed to Him, and He suffered pain and death for them. But God raised Him from the dead so that His atonement also is attributed to us. The punishment of death and Hell is no longer due for Christians, but *God makes His wrath visible so that we understand the depths of His mercy*:

> *What if God, choosing to show his wrath and make his power known, bore with great patience the objects of his wrath-- prepared for destruction?* ***What if he did this to make the riches of his glory known to the objects of his mercy***, *whom he prepared in advance for glory--* Romans 9:22-23

For non-Christians the penalty for sin (death and eternal suffering in Hell) is still due. There are certainly consequences of sin in this life, and the penalties can seem severe. But the consequences in this life pale in comparison to the terrible, just, and forever wrath of God described in Scripture.

Most other worldviews don't really confront this issue directly. Some worldviews say that life just ends with death so the only consequences are in this life. Others say that we all eventually get to "heaven" as they define it, but it just takes longer for some of us. Non-Christian worldviews that have a concept of heaven believe that heaven is "earned" based on good works in life (or multiple lives for the reincarnation folks). Only the faiths that reference the Bible (such as Christianity, Judaism, Islam, and some Christian cults) typically have a concept of Hell with punishment for sins. See the chart in Appendix B for more details.

Regardless of the different beliefs about rules today, we know that at the end there will be no question - God's rules are Enforced.

THE FEAR OF GOD

The Bible often mentions the fear of God. The fear of God leads to wisdom and righteousness. The lack of a fear of God leads to foolishness and wickedness.

In today's church we typically emphasize God's love and mercy and talk about Jesus as our friend. God's justice, wrath, holiness, and hatred of sin are not popular sermon topics. But they are as applicable to our view of God as His love is.

To define "the fear of God" is challenging. God calls Himself our loving Father, and that role seems inconsistent with our normal concept of fear. Yet we're also told in Hebrews 12:28b-29 '*...so worship God acceptably **with reverence and awe**, for our "**God is a consuming fire.**"'*

I think one way we can pursue a proper fear of God is to regularly study God's attributes so that we don't focus only on aspects of God that make us comfortable. To borrow a quote about Narnia's Aslan, "he's good, but he's not safe." As God's adopted children and as joint heirs with Christ we can come boldly to the throne of grace and talk to our Heavenly Father. But as imperfect finite creatures contemplating a perfect and infinite God we should never treat Him casually as if He is one of us.

God is God and there is none like Him. We see in Scripture that those who encountered God or His messengers fell on their faces in fear. We can trust Him, but we should always remember that if we saw Him more clearly as He Is, we would fall on our faces as well.

S - STEADFAST

But the plans of the LORD stand firm forever, the purposes of his heart through all generations. Psalms 33:11

Before God created anything, His law was established and perfectly complete. He knew everything that needed to be in His Word before any of it was written. And unlike man's law, God's law is Steadfast and does not change. This is simply in keeping with God's character:

- He doesn't change
- He doesn't learn new things that change His opinion
- He doesn't feel political pressure to modify His standards to match the tastes of the current society (or as Voddie Baucham says, "God is not running for God")

The rules of the world are firmly established from before time through eternity.

We don't have to worry that God will change His mind and change the rules somewhere along the way. The writer of Psalm 119 recognizes this several times including verse 160 *"All your words are true; all your righteous laws are eternal."* Once you learn one of God's rules you can be confident it will be in place forever.

This is not true of other worldviews. Even religions that are based on written scripture have often added to the rules. This was the problem with the Jewish Pharisees in the Bible. They had added hundreds of new rules under the guise of "clarifying" what God said. Islamic clerics do this as well.

Roman Catholics and other cults such as Mormons and Christian Science actually add periodic "new revelations" to their rules. This allows them to adjust their doctrine to changing cultural pressures.

But it doesn't provide any comfort to their followers to know that the rules could change in the future.

Those who trust in God know that men cannot revise His Word.

*For, "All men are like grass, and all their glory is like the flowers of the field; **the grass withers and the flowers fall, but the word of the Lord stands forever**." And this is the word that was preached to you.* 1 Peter 1:24-25

WHAT ABOUT CHANGES BETWEEN THE OLD TESTAMENT AND NEW TESTAMENT?

This is another of the topics that many folks smarter than I am can't agree on. We're already pointed out that God's laws are eternal, but as Christians today we don't live like Old Testament Jews. So what's different?

There are basically three schools of thought that I will warily oversimplify here:

1. Dispensational – Belief that God has given several stages of revelation called "dispensations" and that the rules are progressively more complete. This includes the belief that God has a separate plan for Israel than for the Church.
2. Covenant Theology – Belief that rules from the Old Testament continue to be valid unless repealed in the New Testament. The Church has existed from the beginning and Jewish believers are in the Church (the Church is now "Israel").
3. New Covenant Theology – Belief that rules from the Old Testament are no longer valid and that only rules established in the New Testament are valid. This is based primarily on the New Testament passages (particularly Hebrews 8-10) that talk of the old covenant of the law being replaced by the covenant of grace found in Christ.

I grew up in dispensational churches, I see some good points in New Covenant Theology, and I probably hold more to Covenant Theology. I don't want to say it's not important which you believe, yet I will say **it's not necessary to believe a particular one of these in order to follow the commands Jesus gave** (when in doubt, fall back to the Two Greatest Commandments and the Golden Rule). I believe there are godly men in all three schools of thought.

Below is a summary of my current thoughts on how I think God's rules are to be considered within the entire Bible.

There are two categories of law discussed in Scripture:

- **Moral law** includes the principles that specify right actions and attitudes in our relationship with God and men

    o   All nations and people are judged on the basis of this law

- **Ceremonial law** includes the practices:

    o   That illustrated the need for Christ before He came (blood sacrifices and offerings for sins)

    o   That uniquely identified the nation of Israel as being separate from other peoples (circumcision, dietary, hygiene)

The New Testament does NOT specify that the moral law (right and wrong) is modified, but clearly indicates that it is still valid:

- All scripture is God-breathed and useful for teaching, rebuking, correcting, and training in righteousness so that the man of God may be thoroughly equipped. (2 Timothy 3:16-17)

- Jesus did not come to abolish the Law, but to fulfill it. (Matthew 5:17) Throughout the Sermon on the Mount he affirmed God's laws and even elevated the standard for obedience to include attitudes of the heart, not just actions.

- Law is required to know what sin is. We are saved from the "law" of sin = death, but the standard of righteousness is not changed (Romans 3:31).

- When the "law" is condemned, it is usually in context of refuting legalism or "works" salvation. Keeping the law is not the means of salvation, but rather we can be saved only by God's unmerited grace.

  It is very important to look at the context of verses that talk about the burden of the law or how we are free from the law. In context they seem to me to be referring to either ceremonial law or to the concept of earning God's favor or salvation through keeping the law.

The New Testament does specify that ceremonial law is done away with:

- **No more need for sacrifices and sin offerings**
  Unlike the other high priests, he does not need to offer sacrifices day after day, first for his own sins, and then for the sins of the people. He sacrificed for their sins once for all when he offered himself. (Hebrews 7:27, also Hebrews 9:9-10 and Hebrews 10:8-14)

- **Dietary restrictions removed**
  *As one who is in the Lord Jesus, I am fully convinced that no
  food is unclean in itself.* (Romans 14:14a, also Col 2:16-17)

- **Circumcision not required**
  *For in Christ Jesus neither circumcision nor uncircumcision
  has any value. The only thing that counts is faith expressing
  itself through love.* (Galatians 5:6, also 1 Corinthians 7:19)

Another helpful perspective is to think about this from the
standpoint of our relationships (the focus of the two greatest
commandments):

- **Our relationship with God** involves loving Him and
  pleasing Him and obeying Him and glorifying Him.
    - The moral law is eternal - we are not to love idols or
      worship them or otherwise dishonor Him.
    - The ceremonial law was a temporary way to please
      Him and to teach people the serious nature of sin.
      We now rely on the blood of Christ for our
      relationship with God, so the ceremonies are no
      longer required by God. As Paul taught in Galatians,
      if we believe that these ceremonies (such as
      circumcision) are still required by God then we're
      saying that Christ's sacrifice was not sufficient (e.g.
      Galatians 2:21).
- **Our relationships with people** involve moral law that
  fleshes out the concept of loving our neighbor as ourselves.
    - The guidance of moral law is needed in order to
      love others rightly.
    - Ceremonial law has little to do with relationships
      between people, so the passing of ceremonial law
      had no impact on the moral law dealing with our
      relationships to other people.

RULES Recap

The short answer to the question "what are the rules" is – the Bible. The acrostic RULES identifies some key characteristics of God's Word. God's truths and rules are:

Revealed

God supernaturally inspired and directed the writing of the Bible.

Universal

God's rules apply to everyone, everywhere, all the time.

Loving

God gives us rules for our good because He loves us.

Enforced

God's rules are enforced either now or at the judgment.

Steadfast

God's rules are settled and are not subject to amendment by men. God is unchanging and His rules will not change.

CONCLUSION

We live in a world that is a battleground of worldviews. Belief in any of these worldviews has consequences, and all of them argue that they have the answers to life's big questions (or that there are no answers). For many people it is overwhelming to figure out how to live "rightly" in a world that seems so complex and that offers so many options on how to think.

But as we discussed at the beginning of this book, there are really only two options for determining the best "bias" or worldview. Either:

1. We try to "figure it out" using our finite reasoning, or

2. We trust the Infinite One who claims to know it all and who has revealed the answers to us.

Unlike those who deny the True God, Christians know that there are absolute rights, wrongs, and truths. I encourage my family and other followers of Christ, as ambassadors for Christ, to learn to be prepared to give an answer to those who ask for a reason for the hope that we have. We live in a world that is poised for destruction (and deserves it), and when people look for an alternative to other worldviews we should be ready to share the Truth with them.

The contents of this book have been helpful to me in developing a worldview that:

- Is sufficient to address most "big picture" questions

- Can explain the reasonableness of my faith

- Gives me a memorizable outline that I can carry with me

Hopefully this outline will help you prepare to answer life's big questions with a Christian BIAS:

Beginnings - Where did I come from?

God created me and everything else just as He said in the Bible.

Intent - Why am I here?

God put me here to love Him and others, to grow, to be faithful, and to play my part in His eternal story.

Authority - Who's in charge?

God is. He is personal and loving, omnipotent, wise and all-knowing, everywhere and eternal, righteous and reliable. But He is also much more than we can ever describe.

Standards - What are the rules?

God's rules are in the Bible, His Word written for us. His rules are revealed supernaturally, are universally applicable, are motivated by love, are ultimately enforced, and are steadfast forever.

We have the privilege of proclaiming the wisdom of God to the world, and we should be prepared to show the reasonableness of our faith when we have the opportunity. We are to be faithful - the results are up to God.

Conclusion

The apostle Paul said it like this:

*For though we live in the world, we do not wage war as the world does. The weapons we fight with are not the weapons of the world. On the contrary, they have divine power to demolish strongholds. We demolish arguments and every pretension that sets itself up against the knowledge of God, **and we take captive every thought to make it obedient to Christ.***
2 Corinthians 10:3-5

Amen.

HOW DO YOU BECOME A CHRISTIAN?

Becoming reconciled to God does not involve a complicated process or a certain set of words. If you want to be reconciled to God you can be sure He is drawing you to Himself. So you simply and humbly respond to Him. Any honest conversation with God is OK. If you need some help you can use the GRACE acrostic from the "Eternity" section as a starting point:

God, I recognize that you are my Creator and that you own me and everything else. I know I have sinned and deserve death and Hell, and I want you to forgive me and make me holy. I know that Jesus paid for my sins and that I can't "earn" forgiveness. I want to turn from my sin and wholeheartedly acknowledge Jesus as my Lord and Savior. I accept, by faith alone, the gift of salvation He offers me. Thanks for putting in me the desire to be reconciled to You. Please grow me to be the person You created me to be, and enable me to do the things You ask me to do.

BIAS REVIEW

We are all biased - Our answers to life's big questions are based 99.99% on our bias, our assumptions about the "whole ball" that we don't know first-hand.

- If there is Someone who knows the whole ball it is logical to get our answers from Him.
- If there is no one who knows it all we have to rely on our reason, which would be the result of random, purposeless accidents.

Beginnings - ORIGIN

- **O**nly Two Choices
- **R**ealize the Significance
- **I**s it Faith or Science?
  - ○ **L**AB - **L**ookable, **A**ccessible, **B**reakable
- **G**uess at the Evidence
- **I**nspect the Evidence
  - ○ Universe = "**Decay**"
  - ○ Age of the Earth = "**Can't Say**"
  - ○ Origin of Life by Chance = "**No Way**"
  - ○ Evolution of Species and Man = "**Lacks Genes and Tweens**"
- **N**o Compromise - DON'T
  - ○ **D**eath after man, not before
  - ○ **O**rder of Creation
  - ○ **N**ames in genealogies define timeframe
  - ○ **T**en Commandments refer to seven-day week

Intent of Life – LIFE

- **L**ove - GOD and MAN
  - ○ GOD - Love God through right perspective (His **G**lory), right actions (**O**bedience), right thinking (**D**octrine).

- o MAN – Love man through proper actions toward **M**yself, toward **A**ssociated people, toward **N**eighbors
- **I**ncrease – GROW
  - o **G**odliness
  - o **R**elationships
  - o **O**bedience
  - o **W**ork
- **F**aithfulness - Time, Talent, Treasure
  - o God owns everything
  - o God gives each of us unique circumstances
  - o God judges us on our faithfulness with what we have, not in comparison to others
  - o If we are faithful with small things, God will reward us and entrust us with even more
- **E**ternity – Past, Present, Future
  - o Past - Gratefulness
  - o Present - Faithfulness
  - o Future - Fruitfulness

Authority – POWER – A God Who is:

- **P**ersonal and Loving
- **O**mnipotent
- **W**ise and All-Knowing
- **E**verywhere and Eternal
- **R**ighteous and Reliable

Standards – RULES – God's truths and rules are:

- **R**evealed supernaturally, not derived by reason
- **U**niversal and apply to everyone, everywhere, all the time
- **L**oving
- **E**nforced
- **S**teadfast

APPENDIX A:
BIAS ANSWERS FOR OTHER WORLDVIEWS

The chart on the following page is an attempt to summarize the answers some other worldviews would give to the BIAS questions. I don't expect that my answers apply to everyone within a group, and this is just my opinion based on my studies. My goal is simply to provide an overview of key differences and similarities between a Christian worldview and other worldviews.

BIAS Answers - Other Religions

	Where Did We Come From?	Why Are We Here?	Who's In Charge?	What Are the Rules?
Christianity	God created out of nothing (by the Son Jesus)	To accomplish God's plan for us: Love, Increase, Faithfulness, Eternity	Personal (Triune), Loving, Omnipotent, Omniscient, Omnipresent, Righteous God	The Bible: Revealed, Universal, Loving, Enforced, Steadfast
Hinduism	(no answer)	To do good works and ultimately lose identity in "nirvana"	Impersonal force	Vedas, Upanishads
Buddhism	(no answer)	To do good works and ultimately lose identity in "nirvana"	Impersonal force	Teachings of Buddha
Confucianism	(no answer)	Make the world a better place	(considered unimportant)	Confucius teachings
Roman Catholicism	God created	To earn a place in heaven through service in the church and good works	Triune God	The Bible, Apocrypha, church tradition, and rulings of the Pope
Judaism	God created out nothing	Keep the law and love God	Creator/Ruler of the World	Old Testament, tradition
Islam	God created	Keep the law and achieve paradise	Impersonal being	Koran
Atheism, Agnosticism, Skepticism	Random accident in eternal universe	Take care of self	Natural laws – not a deity	Science, reason
Marxism	Random accident in eternal universe	Make the future a better place	Natural laws – not a deity	Marx
Secular Humanism	Random accident in eternal universe	Make the world a better place	Natural laws – not a deity	Human reasoning
New Age Movement	(no answer)	Rise above good and evil – cease to exist	God is all and we are all God	Human reasoning
Mormonism	Created by council of gods, including Elohim, god of this planet	Obey the church – become a god	Evolved god/man – not a Trinity	Bible, Book of Mormon, leaders
Jehovah's Witnesses	Created by Jehovah God (not Jesus)	Obey the church	Personal god – not a Trinity	Altered Bible, leaders
Transcendental Meditation	(no answer)	Get along with others	Impersonal – all is God	Maharishi Yogi
Unification Church "Moonies"	Created by a Dual God -Male and Female gods	Achieve physical salvation	God is dual – male/female	Sun Myung Moon
Christian Science	Created by God	Receive full power of God	God is creation itself	Mary Baker Eddy

APPENDIX B:
OTHER TOPICS - WORLDVIEW COMPARISON
CHART

The chart on the following page summarizes some other key components of worldview and contrasts these for some of the major worldviews. I prepared this chart many years ago and include it here as a reference tool for identifying key differences between biblical thinking and other thinking.

I gathered information from several sources but this info is definitely only my opinion and wasn't prepared as an authoritative document. My focus was on identifying major differences, so I necessarily oversimplified my answers.

Appendix B – Other Topics – Worldview Comparison Chart

Christianity Compared to Other Religions

	Source of Authority	The Nature of God	Nature of Jesus	Nature of Heaven	Path to Heaven	Man's Soul	Man's Nature
Christianity	The Bible	Personal and loving Trinity	Human & God – Savior	Eternal life with God	Faith in Jesus Christ	Eternal	Sinful
Hinduism	Vedas, Upanishads	Impersonal force	Reject need of savior	Freedom from reincarnation	Good works	Loses identify in "nirvana"	Basically Good
Buddhism	Teachings of Buddha	Impersonal force	Reject need of savior	Freedom from reincarnation	Good works	Loses identify in "nirvana"	Basically Good
Roman Catholicism	Bible, Apocrypha, tradition, Pope	Personal and loving Trinity	Human & God - Savior	Eternal life with God	Good works, faith, time in purgatory	Eternal	Sinful
Confucianism	Confucius	(considered unimportant)	Unknown – reject savior	Unknown – not discussed	Not applicable	Unknown	Good
Judaism	Old Testament, tradition	Creator/Ruler of the World	Blasphemer and false teacher	Not really discussed	Good works, lawkeeping	Eternal	Basically Good
Islam	Quran (Koran)	Impersonal being	Prophet, not savior or God	Sensual pleasure	Good works	Eternal	Basically Good
Atheism, Agnosticism, Skepticism	Science, reason	Deny existence or don't know	Historical figure	Doesn't exist or don't know	Not applicable	Destroyed at death	Good
Marxism	Marx	Deny existence	Not relevant	Doesn't exist	Not applicable	Destroyed at death	Good
Secular Humanism	Human reasoning	Deny existence or unimportant	Moral teacher – deny deity	Doesn't exist	Not applicable	Destroyed at death	Good
New Age Movement	Human reasoning	God is all and we are all God	One of many mystic masters	Freedom from reincarnation	Rising above good and evil	Loses identity in "nirvana"	Basically Good
Mormonism	Book of Mormon, leaders	Evolved man – not a Trinity	Firstborn of God – not God	3 levels or "orders of glory"	Good works and church laws	Eternal	Basically Good
Jehovah's Witnesses	Altered Bible, leaders	Personal god – not a Trinity	Superior being – not God	Eternal reward	Good works and church laws	Eternal for church members	Sinful
Transcendental Meditation	Maharishi Yogi	Impersonal – all is God	Unknown – deny his suffering	Cease to exist as individual	"Higher consciousness"	Loses identity in "nirvana"	Basically Good
Unification Church/"Moonies"	Sun Myung Moon	God is dual – male/female	Failed messenger	Eternal life with reward	Moon and his teachings	Eternal	Sinful
Christian Science	Mary Baker Eddy	God is creation itself	Jesus=man, Christ=God (2)	Unknown – inconsistent	Not applicable	Unknown	Basically Good

APPENDIX C:
RECOMMENDED RESOURCES

I've been influenced by many authors and speakers during my lifetime, and I didn't try to do extensive footnotes throughout the book because I don't remember where many of the ideas came from. Here are a few books that were particularly helpful in forming my worldview:

- Ken Ham with Answers in Genesis and his books such as The Lie – Evolution were probably the biggest influence on my thoughts on Origins.
- Henry Morris in The Genesis Record and The Biblical Basis of Modern Science influenced and informed my views on creation and science.
- The book Handbook of Today's Religions by Josh McDowell and Don Steward was a primary source in researching other beliefs.
- The book I'm Glad You Asked by Ken Boa and Larry Moody was my first real introduction to apologetics and looking for logical answers to hard questions.
- Bruce Wilkinson and his book 7 Laws of the Learner motivated me to continue to look for ways to make information easy to remember.
- The Art of Making Sense by Lionel Ruby was the first book that helped me understand the formal concepts of logic.
- How to Read Slowly and Discipleship of the Mind by James Sire helped me learn to recognize the worldviews behind the thoughts of others.
- A Whack in the Side of the Head and A Kick in the Seat of the Pants by Roger von Oech were my favorite resources for learning to think creatively.
- Your Work Matters to God by Doug Sherman was an early influence on my thoughts on work.

- <u>Trusting God</u> and other books by Jerry Bridges are excellent sources of good doctrine.
- <u>The God You Can Know</u> by Dan Dehaan is a great book (similar to <u>Knowing God</u> by J.I. Packer but easier to understand).
- <u>The Hallelujah Factor</u> by Jack Taylor helped me better understand the richness of praise and worship in the original languages of the Bible
- <u>Boyhood and Beyond</u>, <u>Created for Work</u>, and other books by Bob Schulz have been great devotionals about life perspective for me and for our family. They are written to boys but are helpful for everyone.
- <u>Big Truths for Young Hearts</u> by Bruce A. Ware is another great family book for studying major truths about God.

SELECTED INDEX

Ambassador for Christ, 123

Bible, 159

Big Bang, 40

Compromise Theories, 63

DNA, 50

Doctrine, 22, 90

Earth

  Age, 43

  Uniqueness, 41

Education, 24

Evolution, 53

Evolutionary Law, 25

Fear of God, 176

Fossils, 57

Genealogies, 68

Genetics, 53

Glory of God, 85

God's Names, 134

Gospel, 124

Jehovah's Witness, 164

Koran, 164

Life Origin, 49

Marriage, 21

Mormon, Book of, 164

Mutations, 54

Racism, 24

Science

  Defined, 27

  Operational, 29

  Origins, 30

Scripture, 26

Social Darwinism, 24

Thermodynamics, 37

Trinity, 139

Universe, 37

TOPIC OUTLINE

Preface - The Story Behind This Book..6

Introduction..9

Who, Me? Biased?... 9

Sources of Our Opinions 10

The "Best" Bias 11

Jesus and the Bible... 13

    Do Not Answer a Fool.. 14

What This Book Covers 15

How This Book Is Organized 16

1. Where Did We Come From?.......................................17

O - Only Two Choices 18

R - Realize the Significance 19

    Biblical Doctrines Based on Genesis..................... 23

    Some Other implications of Evolutionary Thought 24

I - Is it Faith or Science? 27

    Two Categories of Science 29

    The Bias of Naturalism and Materialism 33

G - Guess at the Evidence 34

    Expectational versus Evidential............................ 34

    What We Expect to Find....................................... 36

I - Inspect the Evidence 37

    Nature of the Universe... 37

    Age of the Earth 43

    Why So Impossibly Long?..................................... 48

    Life from non-living matter 49

    Complex animals from simple life 53

    Instinct.. 56

    Man from animals 60

Summary of the Inspection 62

N - No Compromise 63

Compromise Theories 64

Why Compromise is Not Valid 66

Embarrassed by the Supernatural? 73

Jesus, the Imaginative Creator and Sustainer 74

ORIGIN Recap 75

Review 77

2. Why Are We Here? **79**

Impossible Instructions? 82

God's Will for My Life? 83

L - Love 84

Loving GOD 84

Loving MAN 92

I - Increase 100

G - Godliness 101

Made in God's Image? 102

R - Relationships 103

O - Obedience 105

W - Work 107

F - Faithfulness 109

Time 112

Talent 114

Treasure 116

E - Eternity 119

Past 119

Present 121

An Ambassador for Christ 123

Sharing the Gospel 124

So Whose Choice Is It? 126

Future 127

Only Two Destinations 129

LIFE Recap 130

Review *131*

3. Who's In Charge? **133**

P - Personal and Loving... *136*
    Personal... 136
    Loving 136
    The Trinity - Three in ONE 139

O - Omnipotent... *140*
    God's Sovereignty 141

W - Wise and All-Knowing *143*
    Knowledge.. 143
    Wisdom 144

E – Everywhere and Eternal *146*
    Omnipresent 146
    Eternal... 147

R - Righteous and Reliable *149*
    Righteous 149
    Reliable.. 150
    Where is God in the Dark Times?................................ 152

POWER Recap... *153*

Review.. *154*

4. What Are the Rules? **157**

R - Revealed (Supernaturally) *159*
    How Do We Know the Bible is God's Word?.................... 160
    So...Who Would You Believe? 165
    The CANON of Scripture.. 166

U - Universal *167*
    God's rules and the Church 169

L - Loving.. *170*

E - Enforced... *173*
    The Fear of God.. 176

S - Steadfast.. *177*

What About Changes between the Old Testament and New Testament?
.... 178

RULES Recap.. *182*

Conclusion **183**

How Do You Become a Christian?... 185

BIAS Review... **186**

Appendix A: BIAS Answers for Other Worldviews **188**

Appendix B: Other Topics - Worldview Comparison Chart **190**

Appendix C: Recommended Resources **192**

Selected Index **194**

Topic Outline **195**

www.ingramcontent.com/pod-product-compliance
Lightning Source LLC
LaVergne TN
LVHW051630080426
835511LV00016B/2270